BRAVE N

BRAVE NEW WORLD
REVISITED

NOTES

including
- *Introduction*
- *Chapter Summaries and Commentaries*
- *Character Sketches*
- *Critical Notes*
- *Review Questions*
- *Selected Bibliography*

by
Warren Paul, M.A.
Columbia University

INCORPORATED

LINCOLN, NEBRASKA 68501

Editor	Consulting Editor
Gary Carey, M.A.	*James L. Roberts, Ph.D.*
University of Colorado	*Department of English*
	University of Nebraska

ISBN 0-8220-0256-6

© Copyright 1965

by

C. K. Hillegass

All Rights Reserved

Printed in U.S.A.

1988 Printing

Cliffs Notes, Inc.   Lincoln, Nebraska

CONTENTS

BIOGRAPHY

Aldous Leonard Huxley was born July 26, 1894, in Surrey, England. His father, Leonard, was an editor and minor poet; his mother was the former Julia Arnold. His grandfather was Thomas Henry Huxley (1825-1895), Victorian scientist, essayist, defender of Darwin, and an agnostic. A maternal granduncle was Matthew Arnold (1822-1888), celebrated poet and critic.

Young Aldous studied first at Eton, and then at Balliol College, Oxford. His youthful desire was to become a doctor, but an eye infection nearly blinded him, and he abandoned the idea of studying medicine. This near tragedy colored the balance of his life, and probably accounts for some of the bitterness in his writing. It also may have been at the root of his perennial aversion to the human body. More immediately, it made him decide against entering business or the professions, and to tap more purely personal and artisitic resources in trying to derive a living. As a result of exercises and self-discipline, Huxley's sight became somewhat restored, and he continued at Oxford, taking a degree in 1916.

Bothered by poor eyesight for most of his life thereafter, he saw only limited service as an auxiliary in World War I. His keen interpretation of the intellectual reaction to the hostilities and of the uneasy peace on the part of members of the literary group in which he had begun to move proved of much value in early attempts at writing about the enlightened despair and fruitless spiritual efforts prevalent in the twenties.

He first tried journalism. His marriage, to Maria Nys, a Belgian refugee, took place in 1919. They had one son, Matthew. In the meantime, Huxley wrote and published two volumes of symbolist poetry. Following the war, he flirted briefly with the then-triumphant, predominantly English imagist movement.

In 1921, he turned completely to more creative writing as a means of support and self-expression. After two volumes of short stories, he produced a series of novels which were witty and shrewdly skeptical accounts of the mental crisis suffered by the upper middle class and the *avant-garde* bohemians because hostilities had changed the world, but had not improved it. For his sophisticated satire Huxley came to be considered a prophet of doom for the cult of the amusing — then very much in vogue. His novels drew sharply away from realism, showing more and more dispassion and analysis, and permitting ideas to become the motivating forces in his plots. The high-water mark, the semi-realistic *Point Counter Point,* appeared ten years following World War I, and is usually considered his most celebrated novel. It employed an expository imitation of musical counterpoint, resulting in a plot of sharp extremes of action and idea. Huxley was considered at his mature best in this studied scrutiny of the decadence of modern society due to the disruption of harmony in the "whole" man. The hero was said to have been patterned on D. H. Lawrence.

There followed a feverish output of prose, which was combined with a great deal of traveling. Huxley's wanderings brought him into contact with Gerald Heard, the writer, from whom he acquired a quasi mystical notion of the evolutionary development of human consciousness. A greater influence was the famed novelist D. H. Lawrence (1885-1930). Lawrence himself had had a short-lived affection for the imagist philosophy. Between 1923 and 1933, Huxley visited Italy, where he saw much of Lawrence, becoming a kind of disciple, though their respective views concerning flesh and lust often seemed to be at opposite poles. In 1933, Huxley edited the letters of the dead Lawrence.

In 1924, a collection of Huxley's poetry had been published. A steady stream of novels and nonfictional critical works continued to pour from his pen. *Brave New World* (1932) marked a departure from earlier fictional treatment of the dilemmas characterizing our time. Here Huxley abandoned his former visions of evil as a mildly amusing social phenomenon and adopted a more cosmic view, possibly with some loss of artistic freedom. Here, by contrast, evil is overdrawn rather than underdrawn and becomes identified with the materialism and sensuality of modern man portrayed as a worship of the machine and the flesh. This was a theme to which he never tired of returning, as in *Brave New World Revisited* (1958), where it was transposed to a diatribe against overpopulation and overconsumption.

In 1934, Huxley visited Central America. He came to the United States in 1937 and decided to settle permanently in California, where he stayed until his death. For a while, he wrote scenarios in Hollywood. Not long after his settlement on the West Coast, and probably partly as a result of the intense fundamentalist religious revival in California, he began to be interested in what — in his case — has been called "eclectic mysticism." This belief in some intuitively knowable, but indefinable, source of, and plan for, the universe borrowed heavily from many of the more orthodox and transcendental religions and philosophies, especially Oriental ones (such as Yoga). In any case, mystical belief was to serve as a constant and positive base for moral values in an otherwise meaningless and absurd cosmos. This was in fact meant to contrast favorably with the moral dissolution thought to be rife in the occidental world. The brilliant and satirical novels and stories of the era between world wars came to an end. A transition to mystical writings began in 1936 and culminated in a rather complete exposition of the mystical way, *The Perennial Philosophy* (1945).

In 1955, Huxley's first wife died, and in the following year he married Laural Archera. In 1959, he was awarded a Doctor of Letters degree by the University of California. His later works included several biographies, and have exhibited a variety of forms and styles and treated a variety of subjects.

Aldous Huxley died November 22, 1963, in Los Angeles. It was on the same day of crisis and despair when President John F. Kennedy was assassinated; hence, the passing of the writer was scarcely noticed by most. The few critical articles that summed up his career looked back with wistfulness upon his earlier witty novels and tended to ignore his later mysticism and political idealism.

AN INTRODUCTION

THE UTOPIAN IDEA

If we were to survey the body of writings about Utopia, we might note in some of the historical examples many of the ingredients that compose *Brave New World*. Utopian literature dates from the fifth century before Christ. It was early seen as a sound technique for promoting ethical teaching within a pleasing framework which had some meaning of its own. The form soon became quite popular with readers, especially as the fable and the religious and secular allegory of the Middle Ages.

The Greek Aristophanes, in his play *The Birds,* sketched a Utopian city in the air meant to highlight the corruption of imperial Athens. Aristotle discussed the ideal community somewhat indirectly in those of his works which have a political tinge, notably in the *Nichomachean Ethics.* It was, however, in the hands of Plato that the scientifically organized cooperative community received systematic treatment and full expression. He was the first to note that in any Utopia some means of selection and regulation of its populace would be essential. In the search for the common good – or justice – within a system of political economy, Socrates in *The Republic* imagines a controlled superstate where each man's role is based upon a quite frankly biased view. Plato simply accepted as obvious that there were natural rulers and natural subjects, the former of course in clear minority. In Socrates' idealized community philosophers were to be the born rulers (reminding us of Mustapha Mond in *Brave New World*), because they were wise and therefore honest. Below them, keeping order, would be the larger class of warriors, and below these the huge mass of workers. In Plato's society, as in Huxley's more rigid one, children were nurtured by the state. There was no marriage, since wives were held in common. So we see that eugenics and political repression were major factors in the earliest Utopias. But the most critical factor was the hierarchy.

In the Middle Ages, the influence of *The Republic* was seen in the ideal state suggested by Sir Thomas More in the volume which gave its name to this type of literature as a whole, *Utopia* (1516). The name is actually a play on two Greek words meaning "no place" and "good place." Already, however, in More's thought the social notions of Plato have undergone a change. The book presents an indictment of the harsh justice prevailing in Elizabethan times, wherein More maintains that crime is a result of the perverted social order. Instead of punishing crime, the state should correct the societal abuses which cause it. The worst of these abuses is private ownership of property, which breeds envy, greed, and crime. Property should be enjoyed by all, regardless of birth.

In the second part of *Utopia,* Raphael Hythloday, the hero, visits the Utopian island, which contains fifty-four well planned cities. Here, population is kept constant, agriculture is regulated, and the produce of the state is distributed directly to the public at community markets. Love of money and finery are particularly discouraged, and the citizens are taught farming plus a craft. The work day has been deliberately shortened so that everyone may have time for some relaxation and for education, which is state sponsored and compulsory. There was absolute tolerance in the case of religion, but agnostics were not permitted to hold office. Laws were kept to a minimum and were so simplified that all could understand them, making lawyers unnecessary. War was waged only to relieve the oppressed or in self-defense.

A kindred branch of more or less prophetic writing was the religious allegory of late classical times and the early Middle Ages. Here, as in St. Augustine's *City of God* or the much later *Pilgrim's Progress* (1675) of Bunyan, the theme is one of finding individual or group salvation, commonly within a society not devoted to Utopian ends. The theme of Tommaso Campanella's *City of the Sun* (1623) was salvation. The book advocated a type of communism and a biologically controlled society, ruled by a priest-king and three ministers of state. Actually, the scheme reflected Campanella's dream of a united mankind converted to Catholicism in a world state under the leadership of the pope.

The Renaissance promise of science as liberator and universal benefactor sounded in More was very vigorously proclaimed by Francis Bacon in his unfinished *New Atlantis* (1627). There, through skillful research and discovery, an isolated society completely harnessed nature to do man's bidding. Bacon was able to predict the microphone and the telephone, among other more fantastic improvements. Science plays an extremely important part in *Brave New World;* there it has helped enslave man rather than liberate him, but Huxley is always careful to distinguish between pure and applied science.

Huxley has most often been likened by his critics to Jonathan Swift (1667-1745), who has been called the most versatile, powerful, and withering of English satirists. Huxley resembles him not only in being the possessor of a vast wit, but in acting like him as a gadfly to the state. From the *Battle of the Books* (1697) to *A Modest Proposal* (1729), nothing escaped Swift's scorn, and there was scarcely an institution that did not come under his unflinching scrutiny. He resembles our present author in that his early wit and trenchant powers of analysis gave way at the end of his career to high despair.

Almost all of Swift's moralistic major works are allegories, each examining and assessing some facet of public life. The celebrated *Gulliver's Travels* (1726) was a masterpiece of semi-Utopian narrative, and has been one of the most widely read books of all time, both for children and adults. On the surface, it is a book of travels into highly improbable lands and hence a story of adventure. Underneath it is a fierce satire in which Swift attacks the pettiness and grossness of man, and unleashes his bitterness against fate and human society. It is not without its imaginative Utopian gimmicks: a race of very tiny people; another race of beings sixty feet tall; a society of philosophers and scientists (one of whom has spent eight years in trying to extract sunbeams from cucumbers – a jibe at the Royal Society); and a truly Utopian land which is ruled in peace and integrity by a horse-like people.

Another strain in *Brave New World* stems from what might be termed the literature of escape. It calls for that simplification of personal want and naturalness of living that we find on the part of the outcast inhabitants of the Savage Reservation in *Brave New World*. The historical apostle of this way of thinking and feeling was Jean-Jacques Rousseau. The eighteenth-century philosopher advocated an appeal to the simple dictates of nature in politics, religion, education, art, and living in general. "Man is born free, and everywhere he is in chains," announces the *Social Contract* (1762), and for an excellent poetic description of this predicament we need turn only to Huxley's Utopian state. Rousseau blamed whatever misery man usually suffers on an overabundance of "culture" and complexity of civilization. He was in fact an outspoken critic of the smug progressive tenets of the enlightenment in much the way Huxley is of the optimism of the twenties and thirties. Both felt that reason was powerless to perfect the world without the guidance of feeling. Rousseau's championship of the noble savage has obviously found its more modern counterpart in the warm and sympathetic portrayal of John in *Brave New World*.

The idea of achieving perfection by escaping the impact of culture through individual retreat is abundantly treated in literature, secular as well as religious. A good American example is Thoreau's *Walden*. The idea of retreating to nature and the natural state held much attraction for Huxley, though it was unsuccessful for his character, John. It played a part in Huxley's own life, as seen in his migration from Europe to the Caribbean to the New Mexican desert—to join D. H. Lawrence—to Los Angeles and finally to the California countryside. We know too that Huxley was thinking a lot about political decentralization at this time. This was to be traced to his experiences in fast paced Los Angeles, where he came to feel a deep distrust for democracy and equality. The idea that the least government is the best government can be traced clearly in Thoreau and Rousseau.

It is perhaps more than coincidental that the title of Huxley's novel is taken from Shakespeare. The themes of escapism, glorification of nature, and natural nobility run through much of that poet's work, and it is Shakespeare which John the Savage uses in obtaining his entire education in conformity with nature.

Following 1600 the output of Utopian literature enormously increased and grew more practical in tone. The ideas of men like Robert Owen in England and Charles Fourier in France resulted in actual experimental models of Utopian communities. Owen himself established one first in New Lanarck, Scotland, and then at New Harmony, in Indiana. Many of these inspired settlements had some religious affiliation: the eighteenth century saw the Mennonites and Moravians, the nineteenth, the Shakers, Mormons, and Zionists; all form specialized societies. Most, if not all, of these were earmarked by a simple cooperative economy, private property was discouraged, there was much simplification of custom, cultivation of the land and home crafts were sponsored, and family relations were frequently subject to experimentation. This type of community rarely lasted any length of time, and where one did persist, it usually modified its original character markedly due to pressures from inside and out. One of the most interesting attempts was an American one—Brook Farm. Founded about the time of the Civil War, it was associated with native romantic philosophy and simple cooperative living. Thoreau, himself, had some sympathy with the experiment.

In 1872 a notable English example appeared: it was *Erewhon* (an anagram of *nowhere*) or *Over the Range* by Samuel Butler. It became quite popular. In it a young traveler discovers the land of Erewhon, a realm of quite different ideals in satiric contrast with Victorian English standards. In the new land, disease is a crime and crime a disease; religion is performed like banking; and machines are banned, because it is feared they will become the masters of men. In *Erewhon* the plot features a romantic interest.

Continuing in the Romantic-Victorian tradition, one of the most popular novels of Utopia was the American *Looking Backward* by Edward Bellamy. It appeared in 1888 and was one of the number of visionary utterances by the same author. In it, the hero is transported to the Boston of the year 2000. It featured an industrial army; nevertheless it was entirely American in scope, disavowing class war to achieve its aims.

The twentieth century saw a flood of literary Utopias. These were mostly "technological Utopias" in which man enjoyed a blissful leisure while work was done by obedient machines. Some of these were the expression of serious economic thought, as in the case of Wells; however, most were merely naive glorifications of mechanical progress.

It is curious to note that H. G. Wells (1866-1946) studied science under old Thomas Henry Huxley. Wells came finally to be considered a master of science fiction because his glimpses of the future seemed uncanny, even though they merely extended the limits of the probable. In 1895, *The Time Machine* divided the earth between master race and resentful serfs — a precursive scheme of what we shudder at in *Brave New World. The War of the Worlds* (1898) stated that reason would triumph over the instincts of the blood. Wells was a critic who believed passionately in civilization and man. His constant view was that nationalism was anachronistic, and that contemporary systems and institutions were merely transitory and must of necessity give way to a world state. *A Modern Utopia* (1905) was but one of a series of prophetic novels. A more mature product, *The Shape of Things to Come* (1933) was written at just about the same time as *Brave New World;* the two works are comparable, though the respective authors are considered as belonging to two different ages. In the Wells novel, following a furiously destructive World War II, there is a creative revolution, and then a new government of the world under the Air Dictatorship. Despite such seeming bureaucracy, the world undergoes what is termed a "progressive revolution" — science is put to work to level and rebuild old buildings, conquer disease, and to produce many mechanical conveniences. The novel is notable for its (sometimes bitter) condemnation of capitalism as the self-destructive creator of great waste.

Written in the same year as the Wells novel, James Hilton's *Lost Horizon* represented a return to the sentimental, escapist Utopia. In his tale of a valley miraculously cut off from the severe Himalayan winters, the climate is so beneficial that citizens live many times the length of a normal lifetime, and natural resources are more than abundant. Society is based upon the principles of fellowship and benevolence. The exciting plot of this novel made it known to one of the widest audiences. It added the name "Shangri-la" as a common noun to the English language.

The use of the device of describing a Utopia as a vehicle for satire or the exercise of wit is as old as the serious model. *The Birds* of Aristophanes was an early example. When the chimerical element in Utopian thinking came to be stressed at the expense of the ideal, it produced what has been called the "reverse Utopia" or pseudo-Utopian satire, of which *Brave New World* and *Nineteen Eighty-four* by George Orwell are examples.

In George Orwell (1903-1950), we find the true revolutionist-poet. He wrote his satires in a later and even more complicated world than that in which Huxley produced *Brave New World*. Orwell was a radical who inclined far to the left of center in politics. And he was no armchair theorist, but insisted on going to Spain in 1936 to fight on the Republican side in the civil war. One of the overriding factors in his thought was his rabid hatred for what he considered authoritarianism, as reproduced in two brilliant satires.

The amusing *Animal Farm* (1946) is the first expression of Orwell's concern about the destruction of individual liberty. It is a satire about life in an animal community under an animal dictator. Orwell, writing a decade or more after Huxley, had already had evidence that dictatorship was a legitimate and perhaps permanent threat to the political future of mankind.

Nineteen Eighty-four (1949) attempted to describe that future. The work was the culminating artistic achievement of Orwell's career. It is a description of life under a dictator, Big Brother, and a vast hierarchy under him. We never meet the despot nor do we know whether he in fact exists, there being dark hints as to his being only an empty and symbolic figure head. Much of the story reads like a spy thriller. There is a love interest between man and woman who plot revolution against Big Brother, but they are betrayed by a member of the Secret Service. He is responsible for brainwashing the two revolutionaries by subjecting them to the things they most dread in life. In a tense ending, the lovers denounce each other and embrace conformity to the rule of Big Brother. The message of the novel is unmistakable: once a power elite gains even partial control, it is by its very nature bound to advance to autocracy and to become self-perpetuating.

GENERAL PLOT SUMMARY

The novel dawns in the year 632 A.F. (after Ford, the deity of Utopia). Civilization as we know it had experienced a devastating war which produced chaos and exhaustion. After a further, so-called Nine Years' War, the dictatorship wrested control and brought stability — the era of Our Ford.

Stability is maintained by rigid control of the numbers and types of citizens and by the precise regulation of supply to demand. Marriage is forbidden. The system permits five castes, the more imaginative roles in the society going to the higher castes, and the drudgery to the lower.

The population is controlled through adjusting the number of test-tube births and an artificial process for multiplying the embryos that will be lower-caste individuals.

There are many petty officials, but the real power is in the hands of ten World Controllers. Peace is safeguarded through the state's process of conditioning all the young to think alike and in dispensing soma, a tranquilizer, to the old. And for all ages there is the distraction from serious thinking provided by endless government sponsored sports and entertainments. Happiness is the aim of the state and "Community, Identity, Stability," its motto.

In the opening scenes, students are being given a guided propaganda tour through the London Hatcheries. Two of the employees there are Henry Foster and Lenina Crowne. They have been dating each other with too much regularity, courtship being discouraged by the state. Because her friend Fanny Crowne nags her about this, Lenina begins to date Bernard Marx, an extremely intelligent but slightly deformed fellow. She grows so fond of him that she agrees to vacation with him at a Savage Reservation in New Mexico. This is a preserve where those people are confined whom the state thought unworthy of conversion to Utopian ways. It is crude and dirty and so are its inhabitants. There are complications, however. Bernard has long been an outspoken nonconformist. He is contemptuous of many of the methods and rules of Utopia. Hence the Director of Hatcheries ("Tomakin") threatens him with exile (to a remote corner of the earth) if he does not mend his ways.

At the Savage Reservation, Lenina and Bernard stumble upon John, the Savage, and Linda, his mother. From piecing together John's history, Bernard discovers that Linda was brought to the Reservation years ago by Tomakin and then abandoned by him. Later, she gave birth to John, a crime preventing her return to Utopia. Bernard obtains permission from Mustapha Mond, a World Controller, to bring John and his mother back to Utopia. When Bernard returns, he learns that the Director of Hatcheries is in fact about to exile him, whereupon Marx produces John and Lenina, who greet the Director as son and wife. He resigns in disgrace.

Bernard and a friend, Helmholtz Watson, take John under their wings. Bernard is very popular now because his discovery of John has so excited the people. Bernard and Helmholtz show off Utopia to John. He is at first impressed, but grows more disgusted and moody with each passing day. Lenina has become infatuated with John and has made sexual advances toward him. This destroys his image of her as an object of worship, and he spurns her.

Following the death of his mother, John goes berserk and tries to lecture the Utopians back to sanity. After an ensuing riot is quelled, John, Bernard, and Helmholtz are summoned before Mustapha Mond. Bernard and Helmholtz are exiled, but John must remain behind. He is determined to escape Utopia, however, and flees to a deserted spot outside London. But Utopia comes to him. He is hounded by the press and the inquisitive public to the point of mental exhaustion, whereupon he falls victim to the very Utopian vices which he hated. When he comes to his senses, he takes his own life as the only way out.

LIST OF CHARACTERS

Bernard Marx
A clever member of the Psychology Bureau of the Central London Hatchery, he is considered small and ugly due to an accident prior to his decanting; he hates the Utopian system that made him a misfit.

John, "the Savage"
Born outside Utopia and brought forcibly to it, his goodness and candor contrast sharply with the characters of the Utopians.

Lenina Crowne
An uncommonly pretty and "pneumatic" nurse at the Hatchery, she tends to be flighty and sentimental; she dates Marx and Foster.

Mustapha Mond
His fordship, the Resident Controller for Western Europe; a wily but basically kind man who remembers the pre-Utopian world but prefers Utopia.

"Tomakin"
Director of the Hatchery (D.H.C.), a petty official of Utopia who likes to throw his weight around.

Linda
A now decaying one-time amour of the D.H.C., who accidentally bore John by him, and was left behind on the Savage Reservation.

Helmholtz Watson
A friend of Marx, a brilliant and handsome author of Utopian propaganda (an Emotional Engineer) and a would-be rebel.

Henry Foster
A junior executive at the Hatchery, eager and a walking compendium of statistics.

Warden
A boring windbag who likes to corner a captive audience of tourists to the Savage Reservation.

Fanny Crowne
A worker in the bottling room at the Hatchery and a confidante of Lenina's.

Assistant Director of Predestination
A friend of Henry's who helps him bait Bernard.

Pope
The half-breed native lover of Linda at the Reservation whom we see mostly in flashbacks.

Arch-Community Songster of Canterbury
One of the supreme officials in the religion of the state, and a wag on the sly.

Dr. Shaw
Linda's physician, who explains health and disease in Utopia.

Brave New World

CHAPTER I

Summary
At the outset, the brave new world, or the Utopia, has existed for 632 years. Human beings are now born artificially, and family life is unknown, the children being created and cared for by the state. Later in the novel Huxley points out that old age has been abolished and that men work and are otherwise active until their death.

The Director of Hatcheries and Conditioning (D.H.C.) is personally conducting his new students through the Central London Hatchery and Conditioning Centre. Monotonously, the D.H.C. lectures and demonstrates; feverishly the students take word for word notes.

Successively, the student audience is acquainted with an artificial arrangement of reproductive glands and the equipment for hatching the resulting eggs. The D.H.C. explains Bokanovsky's Process. Here mass production is applied to biology and human embryos are deliberately "predestined" to a certain level of intelligence. Those who will be leaders are of course not mass produced; they will be able to do some independent thinking. Those who will be followers and performers of menial tasks are produced by an ingenious method whereby a sole egg is made to "bud," creating thousands of identical brothers and sisters. These creatures will feel both their kinship and their sameness of thought as they grow to adulthood. There will hence be no wish on their part to exploit one another or to be socially ambitious or aggressive. The process is therefore a critical one for social stability and is one of the cornerstones of the police state, whose planetary motto is in fact Community, Identity, Stability.

The students next witness a technique for ripening the human eggs. In another room containing vast files, data are kept on all the individual embryos, as well as a tally on the total number of each type. The embryos are quickly stored and at the same time inoculated with various organic extracts. Those who are to form the future inferior everyday man-in-the-street are treated to a number of other determinants of inheritance, such as a slight decrease in available oxygen or overexposure to heat.

In the meantime, Henry Foster, an eager young assistant has taken over for the D.H.C. What we take to be his enthusiasm soon turns out to be the same smug pride. They pass pretty Lenina Crowne performing nursing duties. The D.H.C. gives her several suggestive pats and gets a half-hearted smile for his efforts. Henry, in a sly aside from his lecturing, makes a date with Lenina for that afternoon.

Commentary

In the very first chapter, Huxley shows us some of the methods used by the police state of the future to control and segregate its citizens. One of the problems of the mid-twentieth century that haunted economists and statesmen alike was that of the population outgrowing the available natural resources. In our time the dilemma could be solved by governmental help and self-restraint on the part of the people. Huxley shows us what will happen if we do not limit our dangerous rate of growth voluntarily – the police state must arise to do it for us. The brave new world has solved the problem and guaranteed against its recurrence, for the rate of population is scientifically controlled and each person has his social role planned for him. It is ironic that family planning in our own day urges limiting the birth of inferior humans, whereas Huxley's Utopia is based on increasing their number to achieve stability.

One of the chief charges of our time is that science is irresponsible and must be legally controlled. In *Brave New World* we are shown the result of failing to establish that control. Science has become the weapon with which people are completely subdued. For instance, man has been warned about the potential danger of permanently altering his hereditary mechanism by exposing the body to too much X-radiation. Unless man takes steps to prevent its misuse, the police state will inevitably exploit this device to enslave man.

In this chapter, Huxley skillfully makes us feel the lack of feeling and robot-like quality of the inhabitants of Utopia. First he contrasts the stifling laboratory with the coldness of those in it. In the clever counterpoint between the glib D.H.C. and the cowed students, we are made aware of the dull wittedness of the whole group. The students are to be given a smattering of information – just enough to whet their interest, but not enough to provoke them to question ends and means.

Because of the brief flirtations of the men with Lenina, we are led to wonder whether some of the inhabitants of Utopia have ordinary emotions after all.

CHAPTER II

Summary
Leaving Henry Foster behind, the D.H.C. takes his young charges upstairs to the nursery. Here it is disclosed that the state begins educating its citizens shortly after their "birth." The reader is to witness a sample of this education.

Nurses alternate bowls of lush roses with gaily colored children's books in a row on the floor. The babies are brought in, put on the floor, and turned toward the books and flowers. When they crawl to the colorful objects and reach out for them, they are thrown into panic by explosions, sirens, and alarms. Thus they begin to associate the terrifying and painful noise with the roses and picture books. The lesson is reinforced by subjecting the infants to a mild electric shock. They have absorbed the lesson well. When later confronted again with the books and flowers, minus the terrifying noises and shock, they once more scream and carry on. This is the process of conditioning carried out on the young of a more inferior class. "What man has joined, nature is powerless to put asunder."

One of the students remarks that, naturally, reading wastes the community's time, but why condition people to dislike flowers. The D.H.C. explains. Once upon a time, the lower castes were conditioned to love nature. The object was to get them out of the city and into the country, thus forcing them to "consume" transportation. It worked so well that they made for the country in droves. They consumed transportation, but they were so busy communing with nature that they didn't consume anything else. Since one of the cornerstones of Utopia was constant consumption, the strategy had to be altered. The mob was conditioned to hate nature but to adore country sports which called for elaborate equipment, whereupon consumption of manufactured articles skyrocketed to match that of transport.

In a highly amusing scene, the D.H.C. describes the discovery of hypnopaedia (sleep-teaching). As a preliminary, he questions the students about domestic conditions before the advent of the brave new world. The students stammer and blush at having to say words such as "birth" and "parent." Sleep-teaching was accidentally discovered when a young Polish boy's parents left the radio on beside his bed all night. In the morning, he awoke repeating word for word a panegyric by Bernard Shaw. It was in perfect English—a tongue unknown to the boy, and to his parents.

That was the discovery of hypnopaedia, but many years were spent in perfecting it. The early researchers got off at once on the wrong track, trying to instill knowledge in the sleeping subject. But upon questioning after awakening, the subject showed absolutely no comprehension of what he had been sleep-taught. Further experiment proved, however, that there was ready acceptance of ethical teaching during sleep.

Passing to a dormitory, the group witnesses some Beta children being sleep-taught. By means of small loudspeakers under their pillows, the children have been given a lesson in "Elementary Sex," and are about to begin one in "Elementary Class Consciousness." In the latter, rigid notions of caste-conscious propaganda are driven into the subconscious of each sleeping child.

Commentary

Here for the first time the reader is introduced to a number of devices which are crucial to the maintenance of order and happiness in Utopia.

The process of conditioning very nearly forms the foundation of the state. Conditioning consists of very quickly following a stimulus which provokes an unwanted response with a stimulus which evokes a desired response. After many repetitions, the natural response to the first stimulus comes to be replaced by the response to the second. Thus the first stimulus is linked to the second response, and what is called a *conditioned* response is established. An example of wordless conditioning is seen in the exposure of the babies to the books and flowers. Presenting unpleasant stimuli — noises and shocks — simultaneously with the books and flowers makes the babies associate the two mentally, and their response of terror is transferred from the noises and shocks to the books and flowers. But wordless conditioning is crude compared to a refinement in which the *suggestion* of behavior to a sleeping subject actually results in inducing such behavior in the waking state. That is hypnopaedia, "the greatest moralizing and socializing force of all time." In our own day, examples of the less ethical use of persuasion by suggestion are hard-sell advertising and brainwashing of political prisoners. Mankind had his chance to legislate against it before the onset of Utopia, when it became an instrument to enslave him.

Another bulwark of Utopia is the caste system, and we see in this chapter how it is constantly reinforced. There are five castes, each designated by a Greek letter; each is part of the scale from intellectual to moron, the Alphas at the higher end and the Epsilons at the lower. Within each caste there is a division into higher and lower types. The individuals in each caste are stereotyped as to dress. They are conditioned to enjoy the role the state assigns them, to be happy with what they have, and to keep strictly from mixing with members of other castes.

Consumption is still another cornerstone of the state. When people are busy consuming, they are forever distracted, and therefore they cannot trouble the state. In much of our Western World today, overconsumption is promoted. People are encouraged to consume in a greater quantity and variety than they need. Industry introduces into products what is called "built-in obsolescence." That is, a refrigerator cannot be built to last for any length of time. If that were so, refrigerators would not wear out, and there would then be no more work for those who make refrigerators. Supply and demand is a vicious spiraling circle, says Huxley. We must take steps to curb it now. Uncontrolled, it will be used to victimize us in Utopia.

In this chapter, the reader is introduced to one of the foggier notions in *Brave New World,* that of "Ford." Ford is constantly referred to as the founder of Utopia and its symbol. He is not quite worshiped as a god; his name serves as a rallying cry for the state and citizenry. The idea of such a being does not serve to further the story in any way. Rather, being a clever word-play upon "Lord," it gives Huxley a chance to deliver some witty slogans. The name's overtones are what really annoy us. Assertions like "Our Ford's T-Model" and "Ford's in his flivver, all's well with the world" make it very tempting for us to identify "Ford" with the Henry Ford of our own time. This is patently impossible on the evidence of history and dates. It might be that the brave new world did really look back to real founding fathers. In any case Huxley never explains, but merely uses "Ford" as a nonsense name to provide a little extra piquancy to his spoof.

Huxley here uses a clever satiric device (one that he will use again and again). It consists of ridiculing retrospectively institutions which we hold sacred today. Thus the Utopians make fun of human birth and family life as vastly inferior to their own ways, much as we compare our modern ways of doing things with those of our great-grandfathers. Used as a Utopian literary device, it demands a much more violent break between past and future.

CHAPTER III

Summary
Beyond the building, in the grounds, the reader is shown the play-time of the children of the state. Boys and girls are both naked and participate together in a variety of activities, mainly formal, designed to develop "proper" social attitudes in the future citizens. The formal games require elaborate apparatus, again bolstering constant and optimal consumption of goods by members of the state. The less formal activities open to observation center about crude exploratory sexual maneuvers on the part of the children, intended to free their minds of any and all puritanical

tendencies and of later feelings of guilt and harmful repression. One little boy who is somewhat timid about such things is quickly hustled off to the psychiatrist. The visiting students are astonished to hear that in olden times – before Ford – erotic play was considered abnormal.

Director and pupils are subsequently surprised by the appearance of Mustapha Mond, one of the ten principal world dignitaries. He agrees to stay and talk to the students about the history of Utopia. The Resident Controller for Western Europe ("his fordship") lectures the boys concerning the banning in times past of literature, world history, Christianity, democracy, and family life. Mond tries to drive home to the students the vulgarity and wretchedness of family life and the home in the mid-twentieth century – so vividly that one boy is on the verge of getting sick.

Simultaneously, we are given some flashes of Henry Foster and Lenina Crowne preparing for evening dates. Some of the domestic "conveniences" and activities of Utopian life are clearly visible. Fanny Crowne (a friend, though distantly related by means of the Bokanovsky Process) discloses her plans for a chemical mock pregnancy and very soon thereafter scolds Lenina because it is against state practice for a girl to date one man regularly, as Lenina lately has been doing with Henry Foster. The state forbids any approach toward monogamy because the people spend too much of their time and energy on romance that way. The Controller carefully explains how shortening the interval between a craving and its gratification gradually destroys the capacity for feeling. He crows: "Fortunate boys! No pains have been spared to make your lives emotionally easy – to preserve you, so far as that is possible, from having emotions at all."

Fanny and Lenina proceed to discuss the rebellious Bernard Marx at some length; they maintain that he is an eligible young man, but one whose ideas are not quite conventional. Fanny feels he's ugly and small and explains there's a rumor that nursing negligence chemically stunted him prior to his .decanting. It is disclosed that Lenina is planning a trip to a Savage Reservation with Marx.

There follows a very rapid and broad verbal montage giving us snatches of conversation between Henry Foster and the Assistant Predestinator for the Centre, between Lenina and Fanny, a nonconformist soliloquy on the part of Bernard Marx, the vocal instruction of a sleep-teacher, and the unabashed oratory of Mond, who proceeds to describe in some detail the so-called Nine Years' War that began in A.F. 141 and created the Utopia. The use of anthrax bombs and ultra modern poison gases apparently exhausted both sides, leaving the people that remained a choice between World Control and destruction. Then came the World State, with its annual celebration of Ford's Day. And we learn that all books published before A.F. 150 were banned. Then in A.F. 178, the state pressed into service the pharmacologists and biochemists, and soma was soon invented. With the coming of soma, men were endlessly distracted from worry. Old age was abolished, because men were kept chemically young.

The dialogue becomes more and more abstract and more and more animated, many of the working mottoes of the state are interjected – from nowhere, and finally the expressions become nearly surrealistic.

Commentary
In a very skillful chapter, Huxley sounds his theme immediately: "History is bunk." Unless men change their ideas and their ways, the future will wipe out with a whisk that entire record and culture that we so much admire. The past will be irrelevant; all that will be important will be the future that is Utopia. Huxley perhaps, too, is thinking of communism's recent attempts to rewrite history.

Huxley's clever juxtaposition of Mond's sarcastic description of ways of doing things in our time with a description of the shiny and efficient gadgets in the brave new world tends to underline the contempt the Utopians feel for our present world. Huxley uses an old device of Utopian novels: he questions the soundness of our values by making his Utopians praise theirs, which are diametric opposites of ours. In the course of all this, we become familiar with some of the gadgets, the function of some explained, and some not.

"Feeling horrible emotions" is the key phrase here. The philosophy of the brave new world is that when the emotions are eliminated, suffering soon disappears. Christianity, liberalism, and democracy for long prevented the installation of the perfect society that was Utopia. They are ridiculed as trying to preserve liberty and freedom. Freedom for what? Freedom to enjoy poverty and misery.

Huxley is setting the stage in introducing Mond. It is the latter who is one of the few truly enlightened persons left. He knows both the old values and the new; later he is called upon to defend his choice of the new in preference to the old. The mention of Shakespeare is ironic, for his works are instrumental in the climax of the novel.

CHAPTER IV

Summary
Bernard and Lenina meet in the crowded elevator in the conditioning building. She starts to question him quite openly about their forthcoming trip to the Savage Reservation in New Mexico. He, however, suggests that they talk somewhere else. Lenina soon after rushes off to keep her date with Henry Foster. In the couple's subsequent helicopter ride, we are treated to a panoramic view of the city and suburbs of the future (in this case, what is left of London). Charing Cross has been renamed Charing-T, the cross being taboo and replaced by the T. It is now a rocket station, and the couple watch a rocket arrive from New York. Their helicopter passes over some of the outdoor games and diversions of the Utopians. The couple alights to play some Obstacle Golf.

Meanwhile, Bernard Marx, alone and wretched, while awaiting Mr. Helmholtz Watson, a so-called emotional engineer for the state, indulges in further reverie. It is disclosed that Marx's small stature and otherwise uncommanding appearance are the result of chance and have been responsible for his uncertainty about his own ability and, to a certain extent, his bitterness toward, and distaste for, the regime controlling the state. Watson appears, and he and Marx repair to Watson's home, where they commiserate with each other over the shortcomings of their respective existences. Bernard suspects that Watson is too smart to conform to the dogma supporting Utopia, even though he gives the outward appearance of so doing. Helmholtz feels within him that he has the power to expose the absurdity of the philosophy of Utopia, but he cannot quite rouse himself to feeling anything.

Commentary
This fairly short chapter helps to advance the plot.

The reader is bound to anticipate forthcoming drama, either because of the triangle linking Bernard, Lenina, and Henry, or as a result of the proposed exotic trip to the Savage Reservation.

Chapter IV introduces us to two types of nonconformity to the state, though the resistance is mostly mental, rather than behavioral and overt. Bernard Marx hates the state because he feels that through its system it has maimed him. His attitude appears to be that where there is such rigid control as there is in Utopia, one has a right to expect absolute perfection from it and freedom from mistakes. But Bernard's rebellion exists mostly in his imagination; he is conditioned to obey the state and its precepts.

He turns to Helmholtz Watson as a kindred spirit from whom he may expect sympathy. Watson's distaste for the Utopian regime is purely intellectual. He is a victim of his own vices. With a mental excess, almost ascetic, he has no liking for the banal distractions that the state creates. He can barely stomach the slogans he invents for the state, he explains. Like Mond, he knows the whole Utopian philosophy is hogwash, but he is too lazy, cowardly, and opportunistic to do anything whatsoever about it.

CHAPTER V

Summary
The golf course closes. The lower castes depart for town using the monorail train. Henry and Lenina take off in their helicopter. They survey some of the industry and a crematorium, where phosphorous is recovered from the cremated bodies, and ultimately returned to the soil. They comment upon how members of all castes are chemically equal and socially useful. Linda's firm class prejudice shows. They dine and take coffee and

soma. They then head for the cabaret which apparently once was Westminster Abbey. Here they are to do the "five-step" to the "ether-music" of "Calvin Stopes and His Sixteen Sexaphonists." They dance the evening out in a kind of blissful soma jag.

Bernard goes each fortnight to the Fordson Community Singery. Big Ben — now "Big Henry" (Ford) — reminds him he's late. In a broad and biting satire, Huxley describes what has taken the place of religious service and ritual in the brave new world — a solidarity meeting. There are signs of the T, blessed soma, and solidarity hymns. The twelve "disciples" in the group pray for their annihilation of self and their mystical amalgamation into one soul. It reaches the pitch of a revival meeting. The frenzy of the members is supposed to invoke an appearance of Ford. Solidarity is finally achieved in a frenetic mass orgy.

Afterward, the girls, who experienced ecstasy, compare notes with Bernard. Yes, he reassures them, he thought it was wonderful. But he has in fact felt nothing, and their rapture sickens him and intensifies his isolation.

Commentary
There is not much plot, if any, in this short transitional chapter. Once again, its purpose is to satirize present-day institutions and to present some of Huxley's witty forecasts of Utopian gimmicks.

The caste prejudice that Henry and Lenina display is planned for the supposed good of the whole and is based on an ideal organic functioning in the state.

Organized religion ("church-going") gets a fierce trouncing during the description of the revival meeting. Huxley, the mystic, has tongue-in-cheek as he lampoons ceremony and show as means to devotion and spiritual satisfaction. By terminating the sanctimonious Solidarity Meeting in an orgy, Huxley contrives to show that uncontrolled religious ecstasy is related to sexual passion in degree and kind. The term "orgy-porgy" (a play obviously on Georgy-porgy) suggests the infantile nature of the whole consummation.

CHAPTER VI

Summary
Bernard's eccentricity has been disturbing Lenina. She reflects that perhaps she ought to go to the North Pole for her impending holiday. She had, however, been there the year before and found it uncomfortable. Then, too, it was an honor to go to the Savage Reservation. She would be a

guest of Bernard, since he was one of the very few (Alpha-pluses only) permitted to visit a Reservation.

Bernard abhors crowds; instead, he relishes solitude (a sin in the eyes of the state) and, unlike the other inhabitants of Utopia, responds to the little natural beauty that can be found. He finds the conventional games and sports a waste of time (—"Then what's time for?" gasps Lenina). He even refuses the soma available to the bored populace. ("A gramme is better than a damn.") He and Lenina are on the verge of a quarrel when Bernard raises the issue of personal freedom. He tries to explain how a sense of individuality is struggling for assertion within him. Lenina pleads ignorance of his ideas and feelings. He, finally, tries to pretend a surge of animal desire in order to convince her that he is just like all the rest; but his words and gestures turn to rancor. He wants to feel just once a strong passion that hasn't been conditioned into him.

In order to get a signature for his permit to visit the Savage Reservation, Bernard confronts the D.H.C. The latter discloses that he, as a young man, went to the very same Reservation, where, during a violent storm, he lost his girl friend of the moment. Giving way to nostalgia, he speaks of it almost sentimentally. Chagrined at what he soon after considers weakness in sharing his secret, the D.H.C. berates Bernard for his bizarre social attitudes. We learn that "Alphas are so conditioned that they do not *have* to be infantile in their emotional behaviour." But their idea of duty should make them *want* to conform. The D.H.C. threatens Bernard with exile to Iceland if he does not change his ways.

Lenina and Bernard embark on a transatlantic rocket for the American Savage Reservation. The latter is the refuge of a primitive group who were not worth converting to the new order. These "savages" are "blessed" with all the vestiges of life as it was before the coming of the autocratic Utopia. While the Warden of the Reservation lectures them endlessly on its marvels, Bernard suddenly remembers he left his Eau de Cologne tap running at home; he will be charged a fortune. During a phone call to his friend Watson in London, Marx learns that what had been only threatened—his exile to Iceland—has indeed been decided upon during his brief absence. Bernard's stoicism vanishes. He helps himself to a big dose of soma.

Commentary
Here the slender plot is advanced once more. The continuing portrayal of Bernard's struggle is obviously meant to end in his becoming a full-fledged rebel and enemy of the state or a self-styled intimidated martyr. It is obvious that the direction in which his anger is taking him is not a constructive one. This is a critical chapter for Bernard; his fortunes must begin to rise or fall while his struggle lasts.

Among the defects in his character, he is given to bravado (already pointed out and resented by Watson). Here, when the D.H.C. threatens him with punitive measures, Marx does not pause to evaluate the situation, but blindly exults in his contrariness. His refusal of soma is typical of his stubborn streak: he would rather wallow in his anger.

In the diversion seeking of Bernard and Lenina, Huxley airs one of his pet peeves — that of herd activity and organized entertainment. The Utopians must all be encouraged to approve the same sports and agree to the same rules; they must enjoy liking what their fellows relish. If they begin to seek and savor independent activities — for example, solitary hikes — they may soon begin to think independently and hence become a menace to the state. Huxley hints this is one more flaw in our contemporary society: junior is more interested in imitating the baseball hero of the day than he is in observing the harmony of life in the neighborhood pond. And the same attitude persists into adulthood. We are told in no uncertain terms that adults are expected to think like infants (it has a remote Christian ring) — when they think at all.

With the Warden's complacent description of the Savage Reservation, we once again have a satire on the institutions of our own day. The Warden expects Lenina to blush when he mentions the dirty word *born*. The savages are mostly Indians who were regarded as too simple-minded to ever be converted to Utopian regimentation. Even in our own day they were thought primitive and were confined to reservations. They seem to have retained our environment and mores — the Warden reels off their "undesirable" traits and ways.

CHAPTER VII

Summary
Bernard had forewarned Lenina that she might find the Reservation crude and disgusting and suggested that she stay at the hotel in Santa Fe. But she insisted on accompanying him. Yet as soon as they are within the Reservation, she begins to complain about conditions. They are guided to a mesa, where they witness a penitente snake ritual. Lenina is abashed at the sight of disease, dirt, and decrepit old age, and regrets suddenly having made the trip, particularly when she finds she has left her bottle of soma behind. When the flagellation commences, she is on the verge of hysterics.

Not long after, the young savage, blond haired John, appears and introduces himself. He tells them he wishes it had been he who had been the victim of the flagellation. He longed to undergo the pain without crying out. He also discloses that his mother came from the outside world with a man who was his father, and who subsequently left the reservation. Linda, his mother, eventually appears and proceeds to embrace Lenina, filling the latter with complete revulsion. Like the other savages, she is fat, filthy, unkempt, and shows undisguised symptoms of premature aging. Linda next gives an account of her first years in the Reservation and her many futile attempts to explain outside "culture" to the savages. She also tells of her intense suffering in trying to adapt from snug Utopian ways to the barbaric world into which she had been thrust. She tells how, in spite of all her precautions, she found she was to have a baby (— she a Beta —), and her mortification. She recounts how she tried without success to convert the natives to sanitation. She tells, too, of the enmity of the women, because, true to her conditioning, she had considered all their husbands ready partners for an amour.

Commentary

A rather vivid chapter which serves as much for color as for purposes of plot.

Once again, the superstition and ritual of a more primitive religion is contrasted with the reader's recollection of the religion of Ford. The filth and disorder of the Reservation stand in sharp contrast to the spotlessness and order of the brave new world. It is hard to say which world comes out ahead. Of course, both represent societies which are extremes from our point of view.

The flagellation is too much for Lenina, and she displays an emotion out of all proportion to her background. Naturally, she has been forced to witness things totally alien to her, and can only appreciate the more what she holds to be the comparative superiority of Utopia. But her terror is real, and it is doubtful whether her display of intense feeling means her life-long conditioning has not withstood an extreme test or whether it is simply due to her forgetting her soma.

John represents the noble savage of literature. He announces at once that he has no fear of pain; in fact, he would welcome it. He is prepared to suffer for what he considers the truth. From his honest forthrightness, an undistorted view of things may be expected. Linda is the first substantial character in the novel. Despite the pure fiction of the circumstances she is in, she compels belief. She is all flesh and blood; we sympathize and identify with her. She is also Huxley's mouthpiece for his transvaluation of values, highlighted in her account of the hopelessness of trying to make two worlds harmonize. Her dialogue — half reminiscence and half chitchat — is the most skillful and moving yet.

It is, however, Bernard who somehow commands attention. He evidently has a hunch and is being arch about it. The reader cannot help but wonder what plan is forming in his mind. John and Linda have served as instruments to pit one world against the other. But Huxley plants his little clues, and we can only suspect that the meeting with John and Linda is going to be more than merely accidental.

CHAPTER VIII

Summary
    Bernard is astounded at the discovery of John and Linda. He implores John to tell of his experiences from early childhood. John's reverie calls up a number of events, happy and unhappy: how he had tried unsuccessfully to prevent a seduction of his mother; how the native women whipped him and Linda. He tells of Linda's constant efforts to disown being his mother. She has forced him always to address her by her given name, Linda. She hints it is because of him that she must endure her exile. John also tells of the stories she told him of the Other Place, the world of Bernard and Lenina, and of her teaching him to read. The only book she possessed was a technical treatise on Utopian society. John tries to read it, but soon hurtles it to the floor in rage. These were the "happy times," as contrasted to the more frequent ones when Linda is drunk from *mescal* and in bed with a male savage. She has tried and failed to become an accepted member of the savage community. She cannot understand its dislike and rejection of her simply because she follows the ways she learned as a child in Utopia.

John tells of his finding a volume of Shakespeare one day (the plots of the plays have been the main guide in his forming a conception of the ideal civilization) and of his simple education in natural ways at the hands of the Indians. One day he found Popé and Linda in bed together and tried to stab the savage to death. Because of public pressure, Linda and Popé are united in the Indian rite. John tries to join the Indian boys' puberty ritual, but is ostracized. He tells of his solitary attempts to mortify his flesh.

Bernard identifies his own loneliness with John's. He finally suggests that John and Linda return to London with him and Lenina. John is delighted. He inquires innocently as to whether Bernard and Lenina are married, and is overjoyed to hear that they are not.

Commentary
    Despite other minor threads, the principal goal in this chapter is to describe the formative education of John and to build his image as the noble savage who would prefer death to the denial of rugged self-assertion. The nobility he has derived from his pagan background only highlights the superficiality of the personalities of the Utopians.

John's reading in Shakespeare is at first meaningless to him; then gradually some intuitive meaning projects itself into his environment. Many of the emotions and actions in the plots he gradually comes to see exemplified in the Indian society. Huxley wisely contrasts the Indian pantheism with the "ethical" theories of Ford; Shakespeare to the jargon of Utopia; and the simple songs and crafts of the natives with the gadgets and gimmicks of the brave new world.

Following the puberty rite, John contemplates suicide and nonexistence for the first time, and the truth is revealed to him that the one supreme assertion of individuality is death.

CHAPTER IX

Summary
Lenina's antidote for the nightmare of the Reservation is a heaping dose of soma; she falls into a blissful state approximating coma, her "soma holiday." Bernard, meanwhile, is wakeful and carefully formulating his plans. Flying to Santa Fe, he soon succeeds in phoning Whitehall and interesting Mustapha Mond in his discovery of the two "savages" having blood ties with the other world. Alleging scientific interest, Mond gives Bernard the necessary permission to transport John and Linda from the reservation to London. Bernard is in fact deriving quite a bit of self-importance and secret delight from his own schemes.

John has shown acute panic in imagining that Bernard and Lenina have departed for abroad. However, he stealthily enters Lenina's temporary quarters, discovering her asleep in bed. We are acquainted with the fact that her image has become an object of worship for him, in his primitive way. And he is soon kneeling beside her, reciting Shakespeare.

Commentary
In an extremely short chapter, Bernard manages to pique the curiosity of Mond, the World Controller, all the while rehearsing his plan mentally and gloating over his anticipated revenge.

John's worship of one of the brave new world's "goodly creatures" is entirely in keeping with his sheltered life. His unperverted capacity for love allows him to respond to Lenina in a natural way. His ardor is, for the moment, undampened by regard for the weightier problem of what is good and evil. It is somewhat ironic, however, that he so furiously rebelled at his mother's infidelities, and now has had the first whisper of temptation toward concupiscence when alone with Lenina at the end of the chapter. Will he in this way be able to come to recognize Linda's basic innocence?

CHAPTER X

Summary
After one of Huxley's typical panoramas of the entire Hatcheries

Centre in action, the D.H.C. and Henry Foster are discovered in earnest conversation. The D.H.C. accuses Bernard of unorthodox behavior and proposes to make a public spectacle of him. A gathering of personnel has been called in the Fertilizing Room, and Marx presently appears. The D.H.C. at once denounces him and threatens to transfer him to a remote sub-Centre. However, Bernard surprisingly turns to confront his antagonist. He produces Linda, who announces before the entire audience that the D.H.C. is Tomakin, the father of her child. She throws her arms around him. "You made me have a baby," she screams—to the great agitation of the assembled workers. John then appears and addresses the D.H.C. as "father"—a word considered gross and standing for a relationship which is anachronistic and obscene in Utopia. The D.H.C. is aghast amid the rising howls of laughter.

Commentary

As at a climax in a play, the reader witnesses a dramatic reversal of fortunes. Smug, assured Tomakin (the D.H.C.) has been reduced to shame because of an obscure chain of events from the past, upon which Huxley has been slowly but surely building the novel's plot.

All might have been well had the D.H.C.'s egotism not forced him to overplay his hand. Had he not persecuted Bernard, the secret of his past might never have been disclosed. Linda and John are momentarily mere pawns in the power struggle. But neither Marx nor the D.H.C. should underestimate the cunning of Mustapha Mond.

CHAPTER XI

Summary

Tomakin, the D.H.C., has resigned his position in disgrace. All of the important people in London cannot wait for a glimpse of John, the Savage, whose notoriety has spread far and wide. Linda has only the contempt of the crowd (after all she was decanted, not "born" like John), but she is unconcerned. As a matter of fact, she has begun to take more and more inordinate amounts of soma, and her death within a month or two is foreseen by the doctor. John at first objects to her receiving the dope, but he is talked into reconsidering due to assurances that his mother is actually experiencing ecstasy in her delirium. She lolls in Marx's apartment, with the radio and TV both on continually, devouring soma— apparently making up for the lost years on the Reservation.

Bernard acts as John's guardian and hence has become extremely popular with everyone. Even Henry Foster has become friendly. Fanny Crowne confides that she was mistaken in her earlier dislike of Bernard. She tells Lenina that he has invited her to meet John. Marx has, in fact, become sought after by all the women and has lately adopted an attitude of hopeless promiscuity. Just about the only one who is not impressed with Bernard is Helmholtz Watson. Bernard, on the other hand, is so pleased with the pleasant drift of affairs and the savor of success that he has forgotten his hatred of Utopia and opportunistically determines to get along with the society. He considers himself a privileged character, nevertheless, and as such he feels he has the right to be the state's severest critic — so much so that a few people begin to predict dire things for him. Mustapha Mond is merely amused and considers Marx a popinjay. Among the other things Bernard reports to Mond is that John refuses to touch soma.

Marx is at great pains to show off the ingenuity of his civilization to John, but the latter manages to remain singularly unimpressed. He keeps talking instead about the human soul. In fact, John is unmistakably depressed at the sight of the deliberate stunting of the lower castes when he and Bernard visit a factory. A visit to Eton provides a glimpse of upper-caste "advanced" education.

An unexpected engagement ties up Bernard, who aska Lenina to take John to the feelies (a movie with tactile overtones). Rumor asserts that Lenina is romantically attracted to John. She confides her uncertainty in the matter to Fanny. Lenina finds John extremely handsome, but unfortunately he has not made a single pass at her. John finds the film they see out-Hollywoods Hollywood and completely lacking in artistic merit, and this fact puts him in rather a sullen mood. Lenina is too preoccupied with the question of whether he will later make love to her to be very perceptive. Arriving at her residence, she fully expects that John will come in and attempt to seduce her. However, he is off with a bound and away before she realizes what is happening. John returns to his quarters alone to read Shakespeare, leaving a disappointed Lenina to take soma.

Commentary
Now it is Bernard's turn. We see that his earlier malice was only in small part due to conviction. Rather, the lack of recognition of his worth on the part of the populace caused his bitter resentment. Now that his ego is being fed on all sides and he is lionized by some of the important officials, he is ready and content to accept the state. In fact, he fools many; but he does not fool Mond, who is able to toy with him until he is finally ready to dispose of him. Marx has already forgotten the lesson of what befell the D.H.C.: that smugness makes one forget to keep one's guard up (and it must constantly be up in Utopia) and renders one heedless to possible sources of danger. Marx now considers his criticism of things itself beyond criticism; he has begun to fancy himself a prophet and is running the risk of self-deception.

Marx's care of John is as the care of a valuable piece of property. It is his possession of the Savage that has given him status in the eyes of others. John has become important as a curiosity for the people and as a source of experimental information for Mond. The World Controller is, it will be recalled, a repository of pre-Utopian culture and ideas; he is able to remember the old ways and he is a master of the new. He doubtless has already surmised how John, the noble Savage, will react to the sterility and confinement of the brave new world. However, in his wisdom, Mond wants to prove that his hunch was well founded; he wants to see whether or not his own feelings enabled him to predict John's reception of Utopia accurately. There appears to be no other motivation for his permitting John to come to Utopia and for momentarily favoring Marx to the D.H.C.

In this chapter, the classic device of older Utopian literature is used to brilliant advantage. Here, a savage is introduced into a new, sophisticated, and supposedly hostile society. In his reactions to the strange culture and in the description of the events that befall him, the reader is exposed to a keen satire on contemporary institutions and practices. Huxley's delightful spoof of Hollywood is a splendid example. Here are the title and subtitle of the feely film John and Lenina attend:

> Three Weeks in a Helicopter. An All-Super-Singing,
> Synthetic-Talking, Coloured, Stereoscopic Feely,
> with Synchronized Scent-Organ Accompaniment

This was written in 1932. We may blush to recall that in 1962 Hollywood issued a motion picture in which the audience was treated to scents along with the action.

CHAPTER XII

Summary
John has begun to be morose, overtly temperamental, and finally fiercely independent. He informs Bernard Marx in very definite terms that he, John, will not attend another merely curious gathering and be subjected to its sarcastic scrutiny, and he swears at Marx in Zuni. As a result, Bernard must hurry to the meeting without his protégé, bringing about stinging recrimination from the assembly, whose members have no hesitation in bringing up Marx's past misdemeanors. Lenina is present, but is in a world of her own, reviewing the recent unpleasantness with John and rehearsing the open assertion of love she intends to make to him. But she is forced to the bitter conclusion that John stayed away from the meeting just to avoid her. Bernard's social failure deflates him; he must take soma.

Meanwhile, we see for the first time Mustapha Mond hard at his work of public censorship. He has concluded the reading of a paper presenting a new biological theory. He considers it a masterly piece of work. Nevertheless, since it discusses purpose in human life, he must judge it subversive, and prevent its publication. Simultaneously, Lenina has left Bernard's meeting with an old paramour, the Arch-Community-Songster of Canterbury.

John claims that the new humility makes his guardian once more likable, as he was at the Reservation, although Marx in reality has begun to hope for some sort of subtle revenge against the Savage. In his misery, Bernard visits Watson. He apologizes to Watson for an earlier accusation of jealousy. Watson readily forgives him, and this magnanimity produces humiliation in Marx and further resentment. He finds that his old friend has also run into some difficulty with the authorities: in teaching his own poetry to advanced students as examples of instruments of propaganda, Helmholtz has touched off a controversy over experimental verse and decadence in art. He recites his poetry for Bernard.

John is introduced to Watson, and they become interested friends immediately, to Bernard's slight jealousy. Watson reads his poem about solitude to John, and the Savage in turn reads Shakespeare aloud. The emotional engineer is disturbed by the reading. But he is not able, finally, to rise above the narrow conditioning of his childhood. He is baffled and then amused by the love interest in the plot of *Romeo and Juliet*.

Commentary

Again, Huxley presents us with a verbal montage which serves to advance several of the threads of the story nearly simultaneously; we get the feeling of movement and excitement.

Bernard has begun to receive his "come uppance" — and from a totally different quarter than might have been expected. Both his popularity and subsequent persecution have been due indirectly to John. The spinelessness and rancor on the part of Bernard stand in strong contrast to the nobility and true courage of John.

The verse of Watson is an hilarious gibe at our own modern poetry. The example given is incoherent as to imagery and it reflects the innocuousness of the ideas of Utopia. It is a perfect vehicle for nonsense.

The portrayal of Mond is a skillful one. He is Huxley, the sage. He knows both sides and he has long since chosen, for better or worse. Though the picture we get of him is only two-dimensional, it has contemporary meaning. He is the enlightened dictator, and a utilitarian. Against perhaps his own inclinations, he has seen that the good of all is more important than the good of any one. He is the lonely leader of our time, and we feel his latent regret when he says: "What fun it would be if one didn't have to think about happiness."

CHAPTER XIII

Summary

The paths of Henry Foster and Lenina Crowne accidentally cross. He fancies she's ill and suggests perhaps she needs a Pregnancy Substitute. She tells him rather violently to mind his own business. Lenina finds herself unable to concentrate on her daily work. In a conversation with Fanny, it is disclosed that Lenina's thoughts verge on an affair with John. Fanny sounds off once more on one of her favorite themes: monogamy.

John expects a visit from Helmholtz, with whom he hopes to discuss his high regard for Lenina. He is surprised when she herself arrives instead. He tries to tell her of his profound worship of her and how he would like to undergo some extreme trial of daring to prove himself worthy of her. But Lenina takes his groping for words as mere shyness. Their rather unsmooth but witty discussion results in complete misunderstanding. John, true to his savage background, has dreamed of marrying Lenina and has dared to imagine asking her. She is outraged at the idea – it goes against all her early training. He finally blurts out that he loves her, and that is the go ahead signal for Lenina. She is out of her clothes in seconds flat. John is repelled by her lust. He first excoriates her with quotations from Shakespeare ("Was this most goodly book made to write 'whore' upon?") and then actually threatens her with physical violence. John receives a sudden summons by phone and rushes off, whereupon Lenina beats a hasty retreat.

Commentary

Almost the entire chapter is devoted to the long awaited confrontation of Lenina and John. Once again, Lenina is an enigma Despite all the indoctrination of the state, her reactions are supercharged with emotion. Once again, she is about to run the risk of trouble because she persists in her attitude inclining toward romantic love with one man only (though the idea of actual marriage appalls her). Her behavior is not easily explained; it does not logically follow from all the facts. Can someone have accidentally put something foreign in *her* blood surrogate?

John is once more true to the ideals he acquired from the Indians and from Shakespeare. But his behavior is scarcely more believable than Lenina's. His reaction to her lewdness is far too violent. Perhaps the recollection of his mother's easy morals and conduct in the Reservation tend to reinforce his instinctive anger. But again, he fails to keep in mind that Lenina, like his mother, is only doing what she has been taught. Huxley here entertainingly represents chastity by lyrics from Shakespeare and sensuality by a counterpoint of doggerel from a popular song of Utopia. In this way the ideas can be broached artistically, without being explicit.

The plot of the novel stands or falls depending on the reaction of the reader to this pivotal chapter.

CHAPTER XIV

Summary

John is summoned to the sixty-story Hospital for the Dying, where Linda is about to expire in the "galloping Senility ward" amid a host of opiates, sundries, and amusements. He is told his mother cannot recover. As he keeps a vigil at her bedside, she smiles at him in recognition and he weeps. John's reverie pictures the Reservation and Linda's crude singing and rhyme making during earlier and happier years. He is interrupted by a crowd of children who are being "death-conditioned" in the hospital. They examine Linda too closely and John snaps at them. On the verge of unconsciousness, she mistakes her son for her erstwhile Indian lover, Popé, but finally recognizes his true identity as she dies. Her last look is one of terror. John exclaims that he has killed her and falls on his knees beside the bed. The nurse and the children in the ward are scandalized. Amid the callous curiosity of the children, the Savage leaves the hospital.

Commentary

The amusing, matter-of-fact description of the air hearses and the hospital room set the tone for a presentation of the Utopian attitude toward death. It is echoed in the reactions of the visiting children, who have been conditioned just enough to be callous toward death but not fully enough to prevent their being curious. Death in Utopia means sudden senility, but no pain. To John, naturally, the whole affair is completely inhuman. Huxley may be taking us to task for our own hard-heartedness toward death, symbolized by our so frequent consolation: "At least so-and-so suffered no pain."

CHAPTER XV

Summary

John enters the lobby of the hospital to find it packed with members of the retiring day shift. They are all Bokanovsky twins who are lining up for their evening ration of soma. They remind John of an ugly nightmare. Miranda's words from *The Tempest* — "O brave new world!" — rise in his memory to mock him. He had used them himself when he got his first glimpse of Utopia. Then suddenly he interprets the words as a challenge. He is convinced that if he lectures the workers he can persuade them to believe in the value of freedom and beauty. He can help them create a *really* brave new world. He pleads with them to refuse the soma, which he says is a poison to soul and body.

Called to the hospital, Helmholtz and Bernard arrive in time to witness a riot brought on by John. He has called the Deltas slaves and babies. When he proclaims that he is offering them freedom, they feel they are being insulted and attack him. The insurrection is quickly put down by state police, with the help of Synthetic Anti-Riot Speech No. 2 (Medium Strength) and the release of a cloud of soma vapor.

Commentary

In this small chapter some of the physical methods of preserving peace in Utopia are described. The following chapters deal with the psychological methods; they form the climax of the novel and they are concerned with the philosophy behind the state. But before we can entertain the philosophy of controlling people, we must be shown in fact that there is some real danger of rebellion, and this chapter clearly shows it. Ironically enough, the rebellion is brought on by what the mass considers threats to its beloved slavery.

CHAPTER XVI

Summary

John, Bernard, and Helmholtz are summoned to a hearing in the study of his fordship, the great Mustapha Mond. John at once declares his open dislike of Utopia. Mond is surprisingly patient and indulgent. The Savage is amazed to find that Mond is well acquainted with Shakespeare and asks why the populace cannot know the plays. Mond asserts that the people would not understand them. Nor would they understand liberty. They have happiness and stability rather than great art, and prefer it that way. There follows a long discussion in which the philosophy behind the state finally emerges with much clarity.

John argues that *Othello* is finer than the feelies, and Mond agrees. "Of course it is. But that's the price we have to pay for stability. You've got to choose between happiness and what people used to call high art. We've sacrificed the high art. We have the feelies and the scent organ instead." Watson maintains that the stuff he writes for the masses is idiotic. Mond concedes that instability and unhappiness can be more exciting than stability and contentment. He explains that the mass of indistinguishable Gammas and Deltas are the foundation on which the state stands. If you have stability at the bottom, you have it all the way up; there will be no internecine warfare between the few at the top: "The optimum population is modelled on the iceberg—eight-ninths below the water line, one-ninth above." In A.F. 473, an actual experiment was carried out, when the entire island of Cyprus was recolonized with nothing but Alphas. The result was chaos. The masses have to be kept busy. Another experiment in Ireland, employing a four-hour workday, brought unrest.

The kind of science that seeks for objective truth is an enemy of the state. The science of Utopia, says Mond, "is just a cookery book." It is so formulated as to make the myths on which the state rests seem more authentic.

In one of the most disappointing passages in the entire narrative, Marx, the sometime rebel, begs for mercy when he is again threatened with exile. He blames John and Helmholtz. He grovels before Mond and has to be taken out.

Mond confesses that he once dabbled with unorthodoxy because of his fondness for science and truth. He tells Watson that he, Watson, will have to help pay for the happiness of all by accepting exile. Mond had once paid too; he was able to escape exile: "That's how I paid. By choosing to serve happiness. Other people's – not mine."

So the choice is clear: either give up one's ideals or keep them and accept exile. Watson takes the news philosophically.

Commentary

The chips are down. It is time for Huxley, through his mouthpiece, Mustapha Mond, to give a convincing justification for Utopia. His argument does not have to be reasonable to the masses, but it has to be reasonable to someone. It must be attractive enough to Mond that he is willing to sacrifice much of his own freedom and individuality for it. He does not have to sacrifice all his integrity; he may think what he likes. However, he may not allow others to suspect that he thinks anything but orthodoxy. Should he care to think the Utopian system bad, he would be powerless to change it, finding himself but one more victim of it. Actually, this is true for all political systems – not only autocratic types. One must have a certain element of belief in the values which are presupposed by the system, or civil obedience is impossible. As Mond puts it later on: "Of course, if you choose some other standard than ours, then perhaps you might say (the Utopian) was degraded. But you've got to stick to one set of postulates."

In sharp contrast to the leveling policy of Utopia, the avowed goal in a democracy is to educate each individual to the highest level possible. At least, this is the theory. As Huxley points out, there are factors working against realizing the goal – three of the major ones being overpopulation, war, and human indifference. These sap the energies and resources that might be devoted to raising the standard of living and of literacy. The picture Huxley gives us of Utopia is a warning of what our failure to solve these problems and improve conditions will mean.

As Mond points out, "science" can be used to support any regime, good or bad (something the contemporary Western world has learned from the Soviet Union the hard way). If we cannot begin to learn to control science for the public good, it will be used to control us, as well as itself. The recent furor among scientists themselves over irresponsible attitudes toward nuclear weapons emphasizes the difficulty of deciding just what the public good is. However, Huxley's point is that once you permit fascist control of science, the trend is likely to be irreversible.

Plotwise, in this chapter we have Marx's fortunes come finally to their lowest ebb. All of his former independence is gone. It is clear that he will do anything to escape the discomfort and shame of ostracism. There is, on the other hand, an understanding between Mond and Watson. They now respect each other, and it is clear Watson will keep his former convictions. But once again, Mond is the great enigma. He tells us himself that he was obliged to choose between freedom and Utopia. But why did he choose Utopia? He is not a humanitarian; that would be self-contradictory. He might have been simply lazy, but does not strike us so. The question of his motivation continues to haunt us.

CHAPTER XVII

Summary
The others depart, and John and Mond are at last left alone to confront each other, the former defending the old way based on freedom and individualism and the latter arguing on behalf of the planned Utopian state. The Savage says that the sacrifice of art and science is a steep price to pay for happiness. Mond himself has already asserted this in an earlier chapter. The Controller reminds John that the brave new world has also sacrificed God. John's knowledge of God is truly rudimentary, but it is disclosed that Mond has a treasury of old religious writing locked in a safe. He intimates that what the old thinkers didn't foresee was Utopia and its denizens: each man has youth, health, and prosperity right up to his end. The Utopians have chosen machinery, medicine, and happiness in preference to God. Since the citizens of Utopia have been conditioned to want nothing other than what they have, they are naturally always contented and secure, and hence have no need for God, either to ask favors from or as a source of consolation.

In the old days, Mond argues, men believed in a deity whose precepts matched their own ideas of law and the good society. Whether a man — or all men — is considered blessed or cursed by providence depends upon the standard against which you compare his lot. Mond says that if you want stability and comfort you cannot allow traditional religious virtues such as forbearance, self-denial, and chastity, or nobility or heroism. Soma replaced Christianity and its virtues — it was Christianity without tears.

John contends that you must have the extremes of suffering and delight. Says John: "What you need is something *with* tears for a change. Nothing costs enough here." To counter any ill biological effects from their complacency, the Utopians have Violent Passion Surrogate put in their system once a month. In this way, they get a strong emotional release without any discomfort whatsoever.

John will have nothing to do with the ersatz methods of Utopia. He grows defiant. Mond tells him he is merely claiming the right to be unhappy, and John agrees. The Controller points out that the Savage is claiming the right to old age and senility, disease, poverty, hunger, torment, fear, and pain. And, as a dramatic climax to the novel, John says: "I claim them all." "You're welcome," says Mond.

Commentary

This chapter continues the discussion of the last, though the disputants have now narrowed to two: John represents the position of the ascetic, Mond that of the materialist.

Naturally, if Utopia has no need for art and science, neither will it have any need for religion. The three together represent the great triumvirate of spiritual endeavors which mark man's superiority over the beast. It is clear that high art, like religion, requires self-denial and extreme dedication, and brings no palpable reward. Pure science is also of that ilk — it exacts personal disinterestedness and its rewards are nonmaterial.

All of these are in fact taboo in Utopia. The people have no need of spiritual pursuits; they are too busy consuming goods. Like the notorious and much maligned man who lives to eat, the Utopians spend all of their available time in a vicious circle of producing and consuming. And here is Huxley's warning finger for our own society once more.

In our time we see art and science growing farther and farther away from the understanding and appreciation of the common man — and so alienating him. For pleasure and fulfillment, he must turn to simpler and more fundamental things. Suffering — the choice of John — will not be the choice of many men. Instead, today, man is mesmerized by a ceaseless barrage of endless and worthless distractions from mass amusements. He is so busy being entertained, he has no time to devote to thinking about the condition of his soul. At the same time he is under constant pressure through hard-sell advertising and public example to consume continuously, and thus to place a high value upon material things. Especially in the West, man consumes far more than he needs; much of it is simply wasted because the economy calls for ever increasing the gross national product. Man is very rapidly becoming a slave to consumption, but there may still be time to control and alter. Come Utopia, he will be permanently enslaved. This is what John means when he says nothing costs enough in Utopia: people do not have to deny themselves in any way to get the things to which they've become accustomed, and they want nothing other than that to which they've become accustomed.

So it will be up to the reader to choose between the world of Mond and the world of John. Neither side is completely without merit. John wants a society of freedom, self-expression, creation, with the drawbacks of poverty, disease, and fear. Mond's society resembles the collectivist economies of our own day: people are pretty much uniform and comfort and security has been provided all men, even the lowliest, at the sacrifice of individuality and purpose. The reader must not be too hasty in his evaluation or in his distinct preference of one for the other. Nor must he be unaware for a moment of exploring the possibility of some kind of compromise which borrows and joins the good from each system.

John was perhaps hoping for such a middle ground world in his eagerness to trade the Reservation for Utopia. His fatal mistake was not to realize that there was no turning back. Like Dante's inferno, those who enter must abandon hope of ever leaving.

CHAPTER XVIII

Summary
    Helmholtz and Bernard arrive to bid good-bye to a nauseated John, who is purging himself. He "ate civilization" he tells them, and it made him sick. Bernard apologizes to John, and the three reassert their friendship. John tells them he has just visited Mond to plead with the Controller to let him go into exile with the two friends. Mond had refused, saying he wanted to continue the experiment of trying to convert John to Utopian ways. John announces that if he cannot join his friends in exile he will run off.

Soon after Marx and Watson leave, John retreats to an abandoned lighthouse in Surrey. Here he prays and undergoes self-torture to try to purify himself. He is happy at being amid lovely scenery and at being isolated. Here he plans to live. He has thrown away his little good money on the surrogate foods and goods of the state, but vows not to use them. He plans instead to eke out a crude living by planting and hunting.

John's hiding place is accidentally stumbled upon by some motorists. And then the radio and press people appear and hound him for statements and interviews. He kicks one reporter out, but is powerless to discourage them all.

Sudden recollections of Lenina's beauty and corpulence flood back upon him and almost drive him frantic. He tries to whip his desires out of his body. A cameraman appears and begins to make a feely film of John's self-torture with a telescopic lens. The film in time whets the appetite of the curious public. They come in droves for a glimpse of John. They beg John to do his whipping stunt. Amid the uproar, Lenina arrives in a helicopter. She tries to tell John something, but cannot make herself understood above the din. John rushes at her with the whip and beats her; she runs and falls in trying to get away. The crowd is fascinated by the unfamiliar spectacle of pain. John falls to beating himself as the excited crowd begins an orgy-porgy. The Savage's self-humiliation won't work. He is drawn into the orgy and finally partakes of soma and sex. When he awakes from his coma, he is repentent, but he is now aware that his endurance cannot last forever. Upon realizing this, he commits suicide.

Commentary

This chapter forms a little coda to the climax of the novel. The climax occurred in the previous two chapters when the intellectual air was cleared. Here, the reader is returned to the plot for the denouement. The fates of Watson and Marx are decided, but interest still centers about the question of what will happen to John. Can John after all outwit the wily Mond, or will he have to surrender? The reader will have to judge whether what happens to the Savage is believable or not.

On a higher level of abstraction, the focus has finally sharpened. The image of John has been gaining clarity all along. When he says he "ate civilization," it suddenly stands out in bold relief. He is the noble savage, but he is more than that. What does he symbolize?

Just as Mond represented one side of Huxley's character, the cautious, arid intellectual, welcoming concession, and in which reason urges expediency, security, and conformity, so John represents the opposite pole of temperament. He is the other half of Huxley, perhaps of a younger Huxley, undisillusioned—the poet, the dreamer, the prophet. He is the solitary artist (just as Mond was the lonely leader) in a hostile materialistic world, beset by the mob, which misunderstands, mocks, persecutes, and tries to drag him down to its own level of inferiority. He is assailed and tormented on every side by his own physical needs, by the greed and lust of others, by public opinion and censure, by his own doubts—doubting but still struggling to believe—and he must lacerate himself and the world at large in order to preserve his pure vision of things.

Whether through Shakespeare or at the hands of the Indians, nature alone nurtured the Savage, away from civilization. It prevented his contamination from the stereotyped thinking of the mob. It gave him a breadth of artistic intuition so that he was able to look deep into the recesses of the human soul and find worthwhile values there, and to see that any thought or deed not in harmony with these values was worthless at best. John's struggle is the last desperate struggle of the artist to keep from compromising with the world around him – to cling unflinchingly to his high standards. But, as in life, the battle is forever a losing one.

Thus the little play is played out. The suicide of John is again merely figurative. It represents the willful destruction of imagination. It is the triumph of mediocrity over wit.

CRITICAL ANALYSIS

The reader who wants critical information about *Brave New World* and repairs to the local library in search of it will be grievously disappointed. One or two isolated paragraphs will be his reward, and even these will contain only incidental information. The fact is, for one reason or another, critics in general have seen fit to ignore *Brave New World*. There is, of course, some information on Huxley, but it is mostly of pre-1932 vintage.

The picture could be bleaker. Much information fortunately is to be found in Huxley's own words, both in his Foreword to the 1946 reissue of the novel and in the entire text of *Brave New World Revisited*, which he wrote as a defense of *Brave New World*. So, if we do not mind taking what he says with a grain of salt, we can try to formulate some criticism with his help.

First then, and foremost, how realistic is the choice facing John at the end of *Brave New World*? If, says Huxley (in the 1946 Foreword), he had to rewrite the novel, he would give the Savage another "choice" – that of sanity. As the novel now stands, he is offered merely two "choices": that of living in the materialist Utopia, which Huxley calls "insanity," or that of returning to the primitive reservation, a course the author describes as "lunacy." Sanity as a third alternative would mean finding a realm where government would be cooperative and voluntary. Social and economic affairs would depend on the free choice of the people. Rent from land would be taxed and returned to the people to alleviate poverty. The instruments of production would be collectively held. Cooperation instead of competition would extend to industry as it did to polity, and goods would be better and more accessible. "Science and technology would be used as though…they had been made for man, not…as though man were to be adapted and enslaved to them." The community of sanity would adopt a religion "in which the Greatest Happiness principle would be secondary to the Final End principle…" Religion, like science, would have no predetermined goals – it would follow, not lead, in man's development of himself. Obviously, a society so conceived would produce individuals who would be beyond discontent, cherish freedom, and resist enslavement. Huxley suggested that the Savage Reservation might have made a good start for the community described. The natives under the benevolent government might slowly be educated up to excellence in human nature. What Huxley fails to mention is how John, having been confined to Utopia, manages to find his way back to the Reservation. In any case, in 1946, Huxley thought sanity possible. His critics were quick to counter this cavalier note by pointing out that the world situation in 1946 looked even less promising for sanity than it did in 1932.

Second, how good is the novel as prophecy? Just what chance is there that the nightmare Huxley describes may come to pass? In the 1946 Foreword he says of his original vision of circa 1932, "Then I projected it six hundred years into the future. Today it seems quite possible that the horror may be upon us within a single century." He goes on to catalogue all of the things he failed to forecast — atomic energy to name a glaring example — as had been made evident by the passage of fourteen change filled years. But by way of apology, he says, "The theme of *Brave New World* is not the advancement of science as such; it is the advancement of science as it affects human individuals."

No, this is not prophecy in the concrete sense, for the novel concerns itself with certain very real and fundamental traits within the mind of man, past, contemporary, and future. It is also at pains to assess definite internal relationships within society, which, if not altered, will result, when projected, in that rigid and sterile society we glimpse in the story. And that is what Huxley says to us: the present-day polity will certainly come to that unless man can manage to alter his ideas, his attitudes toward living, his methods of dealing with his own problems and with others'. And in this sense *Brave New World* is a novel of the present, not the future.

One of the fearsome flaws in contemporary life which propels us swiftly toward Huxley's nightmare is man's inherent impulse toward authoritarianism: Man has always needed to be governed, but latterly he wants to be ruled, rather than to rule himself. He seems to regard freedom as an uneasy and guiltful burden which he would as soon pass to someone else. How else can we explain the increase in movements to the right and to the left since 1932, with the result that democracy, that relatively recent, bolder, and once promising system for human interaction, has found itself squeezed by the totalitarianism of either side into disfavor.

Another flaw can be found in the great desire for conformity on the part of the people. There is a growing mistrust and fear of the individual. We may want to remember the warning of Alexis de Tocqueville about the American public — that the chief thing they were concerned with was equality. They would gladly forego liberty so long as they might enjoy equality.

A third danger lies in the contemporary veneration for science, the reverence on the one hand for technology and its comforts, and the relative apathy toward the arts and humanities on the other. This was a warning note sounded already in the materialistic Victorian lifetime of Thomas

Henry Huxley, from whom our present author traces his earlier belief in science being capable of producing a panacea. The social critics of Victorian progress — and one of them was Huxley's maternal granduncle, Matthew Arnold — were already warning that science, by bringing its revolutionary refinements to everyday life, tended to dull the imagination of man, to wear away at his ingenuity and resourcefulness. And these two strains of thought appear to meet and contest in *Brave New World*. Where science is embraced as the religion of life, as in Utopia, nature is coerced, and we begin to have unnatural man in an unnatural environment.

We may recall Plato's claim that only the philosopher is fit to rule because he sees to the heart of things, beyond the phenomena of everyday life and objects. He is therefore not interested in competing for transitory world honors or for nebulous material goods, but is concerned with abstract notions of truth, justice, and goodness, producing preeminent concern for the welfare of all. This is in close agreement with Huxley's feeling that the artist alone knows true non-attachment (an argument advanced in his earliest novels), that the artist forms one of a true elite which would govern best, or, where that is not possible, would be the best critical voice raised against those who did govern.

The final menace lies in the atrophy of the religious capacity. The generation writing in the thirties had been robbed not only of a polity in which their individuality could be expressed and nurtured, but they had their faith in God snatched from them, with once again nothing substituted. The materialism of the late 19th and early 20th centuries had denied God, salvation, and immortality and ended with a view of a blind, irrational, mechanical universe. In *Brave New World* ironically, religion becomes only a memory (and a bad one at that) for the select few at the top; for the others it is forbidden and unknown, as are the arts and the humanities. Indeed, material progress is still the religion for all in Utopia, and as Mustapha Mond points out, a very jolly one it is, with its stern opposition to denial of the flesh, ecstasy, and martyrdom. And so no longer does man grow within his old dimensions — art balancing science, and religion leavening government. The whole man, in the old Renaissance and romantic senses, has been done away with, and we are left mournfully with the stereotype.

In *Brave New World Revisited* (1958), Huxley undertakes a justification of his 1932 prophecies. He says the picture he painted then was so uncanny that he must revise his forecast. His more pessimistic revised guess is that the miseries of Utopia will be upon us within a single generation. In this work, he no longer mentions the alternative of sanity; he gives us instead the evidence for his prediction. Four flaws in man and his environment have already been mentioned. Now Huxley turns to explain what he terms "impersonal forces" which are set in motion as a result of the flaws. Overpopulation is an example, an important one. He then goes on to describe many of the devices in operation today which encourage and exploit the deleterious action of these forces.

Finally, what can be said of the excellence of *Brave New World* as a novel? What of its form? Its plot is too contrived and too awkward – almost too awkward to handle. Another fault – or perhaps the same one – is that it has too much "message" for the ordinary plot to carry. But upon each reading, the novel somehow gets richer – plot and message tend to blend more. So much message might have more happily called for a nonfictional form. Then why give it a plot? On the positive side, the plot though crude does produce some suspense in its own right. Because it is short and moves rapidly, we do not think of putting the book aside. But the most important point is that the novel form lends itself far better to the display of wit than would nonfiction. And if only on the score of its remarkable wit, *Brave New World* is a success. There is something for everyone in its wise humor. What of its style? It is perfect satire. Not one of us can fail to recognize our worst contemporary faults in the haphazard bungling of Bernard, Helmholtz, Lenina. Huxley is also a master at producing irony within satire: take one of the "montage" scenes, where several diverse actions or speeches will be cut up and juxtaposed, disparate scrap with disparate scrap, and note the skill with which Huxley brings out the irony by intensifying the contrast between the fragments. Note the cunning use of slogans of the state to create this same effect; these do not always click, but it is well worth awaiting the times they do. Finally, there is the wise economy of style: no description is wasted, it always counts; every word is the exact one, with the exact overtones. And in that sense, the novel is an immaculate one.

The characters are representational; the liberal sprinkling of historical names among them is a sure hint of this. Like characters in the older allegorical novel, for example, Bunyan's *The Pilgrim's Progress,* they symbolize virtues or vices directly. They are not flesh and blood personalities with free will. They do not develop as persons, except in a very limited sense. In the case of *Brave New World,* the development of the plot determines the development of the characters, not the reverse. Hence, to ask whether the characters are believable is to ask whether the whole idea of the Utopia is believable. The literary tag, "novel of ideas," has been applied to *Brave New World* with some justification; actually it more properly belongs to Huxley's earlier novels of the twenties, where, in *Point Counter Point,* Philip Quarles enunciates the theory: "The character of each personage must be implied, as far as possible, in the ideas of which he is the mouthpiece. In so far as theories are rationalizations of sentiments, instincts, dispositions of soul, this is feasible." More importantly, he goes on to say: "The chief defect of the novel of ideas is that you must write about people who have ideas to express – which excludes all but about .01 per cent of the human race. Hence the real, the congenital novelists don't write such books. But then I never pretend to be a congenital novelist." This means that we can, in the case of *Brave New World,* only be interested in the emotions of the intellectuals of Utopia. Due again to the nature of the plot, the Deltas and Epsilons have no ideas and only the most rudimentary emotions, and to try to describe these would call for a different, more realistic style.

What of Huxley's symbolism? Symbolic devices there are aplenty. It has been pointed out for instance that the whip represents the tormented battle of spirit and flesh in Huxley and that it signifies his desire to whip the depravity from his soul. However, we might as well shift it to a higher plane and say that it represents his wish to flagellate the original sin out of all mankind. But why spend time worrying about the significance of symbolic objects when one can have the much more rewarding experience of studying the rich symbolism of the characters and the novel's ideas?

The chief difficulty with the Utopian novel (whether straightforward or in reverse) is that we feel its observations on human nature have all been recorded before, in other ways, perhaps better ones. In that case, we may be tempted to judge *Brave New World* a mere *tour de force*. It is ironic, in appraising Huxley himself, to recall the despairing words of Helmholtz Watson:

> I'm thinking of a queer feeling I sometimes get, a feeling that I've got something important to say and the power to say it — only I don't know what it is, and I can't make any use of the power.

ANALYSIS OF CENTRAL CHARACTERS

Bernard Marx

Glum, given to melancholy, physically deformed, Marx is a typical Huxleyan anti-hero — full of ideas but sterile when it comes to action. He is one we clearly do not wish to identify with: his inner conflicts make him suffer throughout the length of the novel and lose in the end — both his struggle and himself. Small and dark, when he should be tall and fair like the Alpha-plus he is mentally, a social outcast, he is at heart an opportunist who greedily seizes and savors the little power he can wheedle as John's mentor. Unlike Watson, his rancorous nonconformity comes from his bitterness toward the state and its citizens rather than from ideals and deep conviction. His loneliness makes him resent even the friendliness of Watson and John.

John (the Savage)

Perhaps he is the most enigmatic character in the story. Comely and fair, wholesomely educated, often moved to tears, it is not easy to understand the root of his guilt complex and his profound need for suffering, particularly since he is often thought to be a portrait of D. H. Lawrence, a man practically devoid of guilt. John's self-condemnation may be grounded in the facts of his birth, which were the principal reason for the enforced exile of his mother from Utopia. He looks forward with great eagerness to being transported to Utopia where he anticipates exploring to its depths a world such as the one opened for him by Shakespeare. He is a symbol of the artist or the monastic striving for ecstasy. His loneliness is dramatized by his dissatisfaction with both crude nature and with refined society. When he makes the mistake of leaving the world of art and mysticism, he finds nothing worth living for in the ordinary world. He is clearly the image of the great man trying to liberate himself from his own egotism.

Mustapha Mond

He is dark, inscrutable, almost sinister, and is a World Controller in the utmost sense. He would never sully himself with physical violence, nor would he stoop to common invective. He is the diplomat and perfect gentleman, while ruling with an iron hand. Long ago he had the choice between his own happiness—nonconformity with discomfort—and serving other people's happiness—conformity with comfort; he chose the latter. He knows the establishment of Utopia is irreversible and that it is a closed system which needs little effort to keep it running. In this knowledge alone consists his happiness. As Mond says, happiness—it's all relative. Much of *Brave New World* reflects the contemporary search for respect. Tomakin will not make a father image: Bernard snaps his fingers at him, and Tomakin recoils from John in horror. Mond seems to have the stature for a father figure: Marx cringes before him and John finds in him a worthy adversary.

"Tomakin"

The Director of Hatcheries and Conditioning (D.H.C.), who is tall and spare to match his meanness. He is prim, almost prissy, certainly self-centered. From his little slips, we can see he pictures himself in the role of World Controller. His rise to the top has been attributable to his fanatical belief and the fact that he never stepped out of line. He would be quick to turn on an imagined enemy, and his vindictiveness would nourish his ego. His age is hard to guess, but he strives to be something of a Lothario. Linda refers to him as a hard, cruel man.

Helmholtz Watson

Handsome, powerful, agile, he is darkly rugged and has the strong features of the Alpha-plus. He is mistrusted by Utopian officials, who think him too clever. He is, however, the symbol of the ineffectuality of reason, because he feels he has a power for saying something important for society, but recognizes that what he does say amounts to nothing.

Lenina Crowne

A voluptuous girl; it is plain that her life revolves around sex and frivolous amusements, and that the men find her highly desirable. But she cannot cure her tendency to want to go steady. Taking her environment on its own terms, she is honest, straightforward, and healthy. But she symbolizes the unrestrained domination of sentiment over intelligence, which proves her undoing.

Linda

John's mother, who symbolizes the failure of trying to impose the mores of one effete society upon a totally backward one. Herself an outcast, she represents the resignation of intelligence in the face of overwhelming odds. Her failure to realize that the old carnality of Utopia was possible only with artificial chemical bolstering results in wearing herself out through debauchery in her own dream world. The parallels between her personality and Lenina's suggest they are both mother images for John: he continues to worship them as be begins to despise them. They both echo Huxley's essential distrust of women.

Henry Foster

Really a minor character who exhibits the complete absence of feeling. An ambitious hustler, he is part and parcel of the system. His main function seems to be as a contrast of contentment from orthodoxy with Bernard's misery from nonconformity.

A LIST OF TERMS

Alphas, Betas, Gammas, Deltas, Epsilons

The five castes of Utopia.

Anthrax Bomb

A pre-Utopian weapon for germ warfare.

Bokanovsky Process

A method whereby a human egg has its normal development arrested, whereupon it proceeds to bud, producing many identical eggs.

Bottling

The process of putting artificially created embryos into sowperitoneum-lined bottles where they may mature.

Centrifugal Bumble-Puppy

A complicated ball game played with complicated equipment.

Chemical Persuasion

The use of chemical stimulants and tranquilizers to control the wills of men and thus make them receptive to suggestion.

Community Sing

A pseudo-religious and fraternal meeting for the lower castes.

Decanting
That process whereby Utopian embryos are removed from the bottles in which they have matured.

Ectogenesis
Birth outside the human body.

Electromagnetic Golf, Escalator Squash, Obstacle Golf, Riemann-Surface Tennis
Utopian sports played with elaborate equipment designed to increase consumption.

Emotional Engineering
The profession whose practitioners prepare propagandistic diversions for the state's populace.

Erotic Play
A pastime of the Utopian children in which they explore one another's bodies — designed to forestall any adult feelings of guilt concerning sex.

Feelies
An elaborate motion picture in which the audience takes hold of two knobs on the seat and thus feels the action taking place on the screen.

Fertilizing Room
The room where human sex cells are artificially united.

Five Step
A popular Utopian dance.

Ford
The Utopian idol.

Freemartin
A sterilized Utopian woman — the majority.

Hypnopaedia
Teaching during sleep; used to drum prejudices into the subconscious of the sleeper.

Internal and External Secretion Trust
The Utopian organization that is in charge of hormones and extracts to keep the people young and happy.

Liners and Matriculators
Employees in the Bottling Room.

Malthusian Belt
A device to discourage sex in the unsterilized woman.

Malthusian Drill
For the unsterilized females – a routine to prevent pregnancy.

Musical Bridge
One of the Utopian games.

Neo-Pavlovian Conditioning (or simply Conditioning)
An intricate psychological procedure in which a bad stimulus is substituted for a good one to remove an undesirable response, or in which a good stimulus may be substituted for a bad one in order to strengthen a desired response.

Orgy-Porgy
A semireligious rite in which indiscriminate wholesale sexual relations produce solidarity in the members.

Phosphorous Recovery
That process whereby phosphorous is captured from cremated bodies and returned to enrich the soil.

Pneumatic
Said of some Utopian women, buxom.

Podsnap's Technique
A method of artificially hastening the ripening of embryos.

Power Elite
A small group which governs artificially by means of force.

Pregnancy Substitute
A medical procedure in which Utopian women are given all the psychological benefits of childbirth without undergoing it.

Savage Reservation
A place where those persons were confined who were not considered worthy of converting to Utopian ways.

Scent and Color Organ
A console that plays concertos of fragrant aromas and capriccios of colored lights.

Sexaphone
A popular band instrument in Utopia.

Sex-hormone Chewing Gum
One of the artificial contrivances to promote sexual satisfaction without conception.

Social Predestination
A process whereby a card file of data on all individuals in Utopia is used to establish a quota system for those types of persons the state is about to create.

Solidarity Service
A pseudo-religious and fraternal meeting for the upper castes.

Soma
The religion of the people; it comes in many forms, mainly tablets. It is a pacifier which lulls the passions and understandings of the people; a major instrument of social stability. (The name refers to an actual narcotic used by the ancient Hindus.)

Subliminal Projection
An image presented to the sight or words to the hearing for a matter of microseconds and superimposed upon visual or auditory entertainment. What is seen or heard in that lightning-like interval lodges in the subconscious and tends to be a powerful influence on subsequent behavior.

Super-Vox-Wurlitzeriana
A synthetic-music box.

Surrogate
A substitute for something, or the thing in an adulterated form.

T-Model
Utopian counterpart of the Christian cross; Ford removed the top bar, making a T.

Violent Passion Surrogate (V.P.S.)
Another chemical devised to give the body the psychological feeling of having had normal sexual relations.

Voice of Good Feeling
The artificial voice that quells any riot by lulling the populace with pacific suggestions from loudspeakers.

Will-to-Order
That compulsion in man which urges him to create unity out of multiplicity, and hence to over organize things.

Brave New World Revisited

FOREWORD

Huxley sounds the note from which his main theme is to be composed: freedom and its enemies. Indeed, this was the broad theme of his first Utopian novel and it is to be the theme of its sequel, though the two treatments of it are to be vastly different. *Brave New World* treated it allegorically; the present work treats it literally.

He is not going to be concerned with the actual implements by which the oligarchs of "Utopia" will achieve the physical impairment and enslavement of the common man. He is interested in exploring the devices with which an antecedent *mental* enslavement is rendered possible and in discovering what factors in contemporary society and in human nature permit —and even abet—this.

CHAPTER I

OVER-POPULATION

Huxley says that in 1931 when he conceived his apocalyptic *Brave New World* he "was convinced that there was still plenty of time." He says that he imagined there would be an extended period when disorder and order shaded into each other, and during which the more resourceful souls —like Mr. Huxley—"would make the best of both worlds."

Mr. Huxley, however, had apparently become a victim of that complacency he repeatedly decried. As he writes *Brave New World Revisited,* he is aware of what all of us knew all the time—his estimate of time was much too generous. Scientists even now are predicting the exact date in the future when there will be no more room in which a person may move, due to the supersaturation of population, and the date they foresee is far, far sooner than the seventh century, A.F. So whether the idiocy of deliberate overpopulation brings about the totally automatic state or, very much less likely, its opposite, or some compromise between the two, Huxley's grandchildren in fact are likely to witness the outcome.

Huxley takes a sideswipe at Orwell in developing his case. Citing the passing of Nazism and Stalinism, he suggests that the more contemporary picture of government inclines away from purely terroristic methods of control and leans toward the regimentation and enslavement of men by nonviolent means.

The kind of stability through punishment welding the society in *Nineteen Eighty-Four* was a pretty precarious one; you always had to be watching it, anticipating. Men were totally intimidated, but they were still left with their ambitions and desires. In the polity of *Brave New World* with its technique of nonviolent conditioning and propaganda, you could afford to take it somewhat easier — sit back and really savor the final extinction of human nature.

While it is patently true that systems of incentives as means of control have become more popular in Russia and Communist China, their use has not eliminated concomitant police methods. Huxley finds the unacknowledged but very real social hierarchies in the two present-day autocracies prototypes of the stratified populace of *Brave New World*.

Huxley turns to what he calls "impersonal forces" which are unceasingly at work to bring about the totalitarian nightmare of the future. These form the real crux of the problem, and man is impotent before them because they take their origin from certain proclivities within man himself. Since man is stuck with his own nature, he is going to have to bow before the inevitable consequences.

The first consequence is overpopulation, with its attendant and derivative evils. As old Thomas Henry Huxley, Aldous' grandfather, put it in an age of laissez faire and free enterprise:

So long as unlimited multiplication goes on, no social organization which has ever been developed, or is likely to be devised, no fiddle-faddling with the distribution of wealth, will deliver society from the tendency to be destroyed by the reproduction within itself in its intensest form, of that struggle for existence the limitation of which is the object of society. ("The Struggle for Existence in Human Society," 1888)

Old Thomas Henry saw, with Malthus and Darwin, that the elimination of war, the conquest of disease, and the amelioration of the conditions of labor would result in a surfeit of population and a lowering of standards for all. Our author says that even were men desirous of practicing birth control out of manifest necessity (they are not), the mechanical means would still be beyond their reach. Church and state are mostly indifferent. Says Huxley: "Even the poorest government is rich enough to provide its subjects with a substantial measure of death control. Birth control is a very different matter."

After some statistics, Huxley explodes the fiction of possible future emigrations to the moon or — in his example — Mars to siphon off the excess population. He reminds us that when the "Utopia" of his *Brave New World* becomes a fact the ratio of people to resources will be rigidly controlled.

He says that in an effort to stimulate underdeveloped regions, public health has been improved; but this has resulted in a sharp increase in the birth rate and a further drain on an already poor economy. "Overpopulation leads to economic insecurity and social unrest. Unrest and insecurity lead to more control by central governments and an increase of their power." Moreover, this economic imbalance is an incentive to war, since underdeveloped countries are ready to risk conquest for material gain. The constant threat of war, "permanent crisis," is added impetus to the extension of greater control by centralized authority. And we are off – to Utopia.

CHAPTER II

QUANTITY, QUALITY, MORALITY

Huxley pursues the same subject. In the Utopia of *Brave New World,* reproduction is by test tube. The stereotyped subhumans can have the emotional pleasures of physical love without the contingent alleged drawbacks.

Sounding not a little like Nietzsche, Huxley observes we do nothing to further scientific breeding. As a consequence, through overpopulation and permitting the biologically unsound to procreate, we are constantly lowering the collective standard of our mental capacities and our physical prowess. If we do not voluntarily do something about eugenics, it will have to be done for us – and to us – come Utopia. Drugs which we invent to support life, he points out, may actually be the instruments perpetuating and aggravating invalidism.

It might very well seem that every invention and improvement for the betterment of mankind, in a larger view, is an instrument for his ultimate destruction. Says Huxley: "We are on the horns of an ethical dilemma, and to find the middle way will require all our intelligence and all our good will."

CHAPTER III

OVER-ORGANIZATION

A second consequence of man's basic nature is his tendency toward overorganization. It is another one of the major problems of our time, particularly in the West, and it is one of the archenemies of freedom. What would be the energies of business and government are sapped by their own bureaucratic methods.

We are justifiably proud of our technological progress through the ages. But more and more it demands an ever-spiraling price from us. As more and more of us want more and more done for us in our everyday life, mass production and mass distribution become increasingly concentrated in fewer hands. The independent man may be forced to turn from his own production to labor for some larger producer. Citing C. Wright Mills, Huxley reminds us that the power elite very nearly exploits us, directly, through control of the means of production, and indirectly, by economic determination of what and how we think.

Where production is undertaken by a multiplicity of scattered and discrete little businesses, we may expect to find a comparatively unassuming central government and many strong local governments. But where big business is the rule, the central government must proliferate and become more powerful in order to regulate relations among the corporate giants and to keep them from really destroying the little man.

What about the individual? Were he resourceful enough to modify his standard of keeping up with the Joneses and simplifying his wants by fore-going some of the trappings of suburbia, such as several cars, a grand house, a swimming pool, and the like, he might again be able to produce to meet many of his own needs. But as long as he persists in conspicuous consumption, he must work for big business, for only it will pay him the large stipend he needs. In his battle for money and status, in a job to which he is subconsciously indifferent, for rewards of which he basically disapproves, his chief compensation is a growing mental illness.

In searching for an image of mental health, Huxley says these individuals "are normal not in what may be called the absolute sense of the word; they are normal only in relation to a profoundly abnormal society." Because of their enslavement to the same material possessions as all their neighbors, they have lost their individuality.

Calling it the "Will to Order," Huxley denounces the notion that the relentless organizing of multiplicity into unity is unqualifiedly good. As some organization produced the social and political climate in which liberty could develop, so too much organization will bring about an atmosphere which destroys liberty.

Says Huxley, man is not a strictly social animal. Unlike, say, the social insects, man is born with too much individuality to be completely gregarious. And man cannot through overorganization transform his organization — his piece of social machinery — into a perfect, harmonious, and dynamic social organism. His concentrated efforts in this direction will produce only the zombi-like society of *Brave New World*.

Huxley next cites William Whyte and the notion of a Social Ethic replacing the traditional ethical system. He gives a number of the new ethical catchphrases, most of them smacking of groupism and the losing of the individual in the coterie. He says the Social Ethic amounts to a mere apologetic for the dilemma in which the destruction of humanism has left us. Its precepts are grounded in the kind of comfort which derives from the unabashed recognition of the safety in numbers.

The purpose of a society is to promote as full a flowering of the individuals within it as possible. To put the society before the individual, as in the autocracies of today or in Huxley's Utopia, is to confuse ends and means. Where society is so ordered, nobody wins. Mustapha Mond is as much a victim of the system as any Beta minus.

Huxley anticipates a new kind of dark age in which everyone is bound by caste and there is no social fluidity whatsoever—a dark age from which no Renaissance will ever occur.

CHAPTER IV

PROPAGANDA IN A DEMOCRATIC SOCIETY

The history of democracy in western Europe and America is a testimonial to the effect that men are capable of governing themselves with some success. But if a land has long known despotism or is economically immature, it must be gently helped toward democracy. For democracy to be highly successful, people must be taught to reason. And that democratic institutions will persist indefinitely cannot be passively assumed, for impersonal forces which tend to undermine it are always present. Many of these spring from man's infinite capacity for laziness.

There are two kinds of propaganda—harmful and beneficial. The latter is rational and acts as a guide in developing that enlightened self-interest that forms the foundation of democracy. The former, on the other hand, is irrational, appeals to the passions, and is utilized to subvert the ends of democracy and ultimately democracy itself. Beneficial propaganda is used to promote action. Harmful propaganda merely instills passion.

Beneficial propaganda employs logical arguments based upon a consensus of what the truth is. Harmful propaganda relies on emotional appeals and distortions of the facts. Every person has the capacity to be swayed by both types. It is almost always difficult to uncover and promulgate the truth in a democracy, where social and political institutions are so complex. But men like Jefferson had unshakable faith in universal education as the preserver of democracy. Huxley quotes him: "The people cannot be safe without information. Where the press is free, and every man able to read, all is safe."

Education in a democracy depends on the unceasing dissemination of truth by mass communications. As long as the press, radio, television, and films are genuinely unconstrained, we may expect liberty to thrive. These media, however, can be deadly weapons in the hands of a despot who censors everything but what suits the interest of his own regime. In the West, particularly America, public information has latterly come more and more into the hands of syndicates and networks, which in turn are controlled by the power elite. This "economic censorship" is too sophisticated to purvey harmful propaganda, and what it takes to be its self-interest precludes its offering of good propaganda. What it disseminates is the unreal and the irrelevant to eternally distract the citizen and thus keep him from thinking about the very serious issues involved in good self-government.

Little by little, liberty slips away, without any seeming benefit to anyone. That is why, in the "Utopia" of *Brave New World,* where liberty has long, long since disappeared, the Gammas, Deltas, and Epsilons are provided with continuous distractions.

CHAPTER V

PROPAGANDA UNDER A DICTATORSHIP

One of the perennial fears of modern man, whether it be realistic or not, is that he will one day be ruled by machines. It has come very close to that state of things in *Nineteen Eighty-Four,* where Big Brother is almost certainly a mythical head of the ruling hierarchy, and also in *Brave New World,* where Ford is long since gone but not forgotten. Huxley observes that the Soviets and Communistic Chinese are on the way to brainwashing their leaders into automatons — whereupon rule by "machine" will be an actuality.

Huxley suggests that Adolf Hitler failed because he had to have, after all, a hierarchy of human beings under him. Conditioning in the dictatorships of the past was by trial and error. Still Hitler understood and employed the phenomenon of mass hysteria. His notions of mass politics were shrewdly articulated in his autobiography.

The demagogue must appeal to the unconscious drives of the mass. Says Huxley, "Assembled in a crowd, people lose their powers of reasoning and their capacity for moral choice." Hitler was a master in that he realized the value of motivation in maneuvering people through their anxieties and fears. The intellectual maintains a healthy disrespect for this brand of herd poison, but his rebelliousness is rendered ineffectual due to the sheer weight of numbers arrayed against him. If the intellectuals openly ridicule the demagogue and his propaganda, they must be "shouted down or...liquidated."

CHAPTER VI

THE ARTS OF SELLING

Huxley turns to consumerism and motivation research. One of the symptoms of our contemporary malaise in the West is the rate at which we consume. And this leads to the strong suspicion that the brave new world is just around the corner, because consumption is one of the bulwarks of that society.

Huxley says that where shortsighted and greedy men are bent upon mass production, we must necessarily have mass consumption by way of response. The citizenry reads a book like *The Hidden Persuaders* and is not even aroused by the propagandistic methods used to exploit the individual. The motivation analysis of the big businessman is remarkably similar to that of the dictator. Both depend for effect on the lowest instinctual depths of men's minds. The fact that people respond so willingly to the one type ought to serve as a warning alarm that they will likely be receptive to the latter. We can give our rational faculty some needed healthful exercise by striving to be critical rather than complacent about the welter of commercial verbiage that confronts us every day.

Irrational propaganda can make a man who always skipped breakfast learn to love cereal; similarly irrational propaganda can change our latent love for a certain segment of the populace to active hate. The difference is merely one of degree. Because in the case of children the powers of reasoning have not yet begun to mature, they are the best targets for commercial propaganda, particularly in the West, where the family group is child-oriented. Coupling the eating of cereal with images of baseball stars will force the already over consuming parents to buy still more. The bombardment of mass advertising and the vying of children among themselves to acquire gadgets and "giveaways" as symbols of status will easily instill in the youthful plastic mind a fixation toward consumption. Similarly, if you want to propagandize for totalitarianism, start by organizing the young. They'll grow up to eschew democracy for the rest of their days.

Most people know there is not an iota of difference between products A and B, but bombard them with enough symbolizations for a sufficient length of time and they'll swear by one or the other. Before the era of mass communication, the citizen was spared all this ballyhoo. He lived simply and he consumed simply, buying only what he was convinced he needed — without being "persuaded." To create a demand for a product in the first place, you must play upon people's hopes and fears. The girl who is told she's missing happiness because of her "bad" skin will easily buy every beauty preparation, good or worthless, that one can expose her to. Says Huxley, we do not buy the product, we buy the symbols that represent it.

For successful democracy, there must be an unlimited flow of knowledge. It is vitally important that the voting public be given the truth about issues and candidates. Yet in the United States, for example, campaigns are orgies of defamation and myth, where both the major parties persuade the voting public that their respective candidates stand for all things. Hence, the electorate believes it is practicing intelligent self-government when it votes for one of the candidates purely on the basis of his personality.

CHAPTER VII

BRAINWASHING

Sometime around 1900, Ivan Pavlov, a Russian scientist, noticed that slight abnormalities in digestion occurred in laboratory animals when some contingency developed in the experimental environment. Further investigation showed that aboriginal natural links between stimuli and their specific responses might be broken in a comparatively short time by establishing a substitute man made conditioned reflex. Hence, it became apparent that it might also be possible to manipulate man's environment as well as man's adaptive responses to it pretty much to suit the manipulator's purpose. Pavlov's work had a few other implications: he found that repeated variation of stimulus to response resulted in disorientation and hysteria and, finally, catatonic stupor, and that the animals showed a whole spectrum of susceptibility to experimental neurosis. Pavlov's findings had an important influence on learning and on experimental psychology, especially behaviorism, which Huxley turns to later.

Very subtle psychological processes were at work. Where the response was one of fear, it was commonly found that the stimulus which originally triggered it did not have to be present at all after a time; certain other objects, or a situational grouping of objects, would come to symbolize the stimulus and evoke the given reaction, in this illustration fear. Under repeated stress in World War I the soldiers experienced shell shock, and in World War II they were relieved due to battle fatigue. The average man under stress reaches his breaking point in about thirty days.

In the dim past of classical and medieval times, you might torture the flesh of a man to get him to do your will, but frequently he was strong enough to hold out and simply died. It is much more effective to proceed to break down the central nervous system of your victim. The thing to do is to produce nervous exhaustion almost to the point of collapse, whereupon you will find you have a victim infinitely susceptible to suggestion. Then proceed by means of suggestion to instill new behavior patterns — patterns which, having been implanted under great stress, will prove ineradicable.

Since the war, we have seen these very methods used for "peaceful" purposes. Political prisoners have been made to "confess" they were "spies." The same methods are being used by the Chinese in their conditioning centers to brainwash the upcoming Communist elite.

In *Nineteen Eighty-Four,* we have brainwashing not yet perfected, and hence reinforced by "the systematic use of violence." In *Brave New World,* brainwashing is an absolute art–there is no such vulgarity as violence.

CHAPTER VIII

CHEMICAL PERSUASION

In a somewhat literal and thankfully short though witty chapter, Huxley turns to what he calls "chemical persuasion." He reminds us that in his brave new world there was no alcohol, tobacco, or contraband narcotics. Instead, there was soma. As Huxley points out, historically soma was an actual soporific used by the ancient Hindus in their religious rituals. Huxley's hypothetical counterpart had certain superior features. A modicum brought euphoria, while a greater dose induced blissful disorientation and then sweet, restorative sleep. And the best part was that it had no deleterious side effects whatsoever In *Brave New World,* such a drug was one of the principal tools for the control of Utopia. It kept the people uninterruptedly distracted and contented and prevented insurrection.

In 1931, Huxley says, the study of brain chemistry was largely ignored. Its efficacy as an instrument for the benefit (as well as the harm) of mankind, however, was soon recognized by "divinely disinterested science." In 1958, biochemical and psychopharmacological research had reached such a point that neurology was a comparatively perfected exact discipline, awaiting the beck of healer and tyrant alike.

Unlike the narcotics of the past, which deteriorated both mind and body, we have today the tranquilizers, stimulants, and hallucinants. They produce addiction, but only the kind that cannot harm the organism. They do heighten suggestibility, however, and hence can be used to promote indoctrination.

In lashing out at contemporary complacent America, Huxley observes that any demagogue who wishes to put these drugs to ulterior use will meet with no popular resistance. Everyone today is so pledged to escapism that the demand for stimulants and tranquilizers is staggering. Just make them as cheap as aspirin and offer them without a prescription, says Huxley, and our society will consume them without stint. He then delivers the United States a crushing blow which has significance for our immediate time, not the seventh century A.F. In contrasting the United States to the Soviet Union, he proclaims:

> In a contest between two populations, one of which is being constantly stimulated by threats and promises, constantly directed by one-pointed propaganda, while the other is no less constantly being distracted by television and tranquilized by Miltown, which of the opponents is more likely to come out on top?

Huxley averred in a recent article that the optimal use of hallucinogenic drugs, such as LSD (lysergic diethylamide), is to expand the consciousness, to make it more mature and hence more susceptible to reason and to the more sophisticated ideas upon which human culture has so long rested.

CHAPTER IX

SUBCONSCIOUS PERSUASION

Extraconscious perception has been a subject of experiment since before 1920, when one of Freud's mentors experimented on his subjects with the tachistoscope. He discovered, much to his surprise, that most people tend to learn a great deal that is peripheral to what they consciously absorb.

What might have proved a tremendous tool for the edification and enlightenment of man became in the hands of the charlatans of business management an instrument for the manipulation and exploitation of men's minds. Referred to as "subliminal projection" after the technique had been "angled" by the technologists, in a hilarious passage Huxley describes its possible use as a sales weapon in the hands of Madison Avenue and Hollywood. Motivational research proposed to sell the businessman's product where not even the remotest demand had existed for it beforehand.

By superimposing an imperative commercial message upon the image on a television or movie screen for perhaps a microsecond, at a really crucial and compelling point in the drama being shown, it was alleged by consumer research that big business would be able to sell everything to everyone. It was also proposed to employ subliminal auditory messages in places of mass entertainment as a means of sales persuasion. This kind of mercantile chicanery was actually tried, but the results were somewhat disappointing, and the method was not much pursued along commercial lines.

Isn't there another, more deadly application, of course? Certainly, the propagandistic. In the case of the more docile mind, there will be no problem. But to indoctrinate the man who is accustomed to thinking independently subliminal persuasion may finally do the trick. This man can reason against and thus combat the propaganda that he sees and hears, but his reason is powerless against the lies and misconceptions that reach him subliminally.

Advertisers have long known that you can help sell lumber or coal if your calendar art advertisement features a bathing beauty. This persuasion by association has been subjected to subliminal experimentation under the sponsorship of the National Institutes of Health and "it was found that a person's feelings about some consciously seen image could be modified by associating it, on the subconscious level, with another image, or, better still, with value-bearing words."

Huxley comes very near to describing the "feelies" of his far-off Utopia when he amusingly recounts an application of this subliminal suggestion to today's motion picture, though he maintains that the omission of subliminal projection from *Brave New World* was a bad oversight.

This particular chapter may not advance the thread of the argument very markedly, but it is replete with those sinister asides that mark the old Huxley at his witty best.

CHAPTER X

HYPNOPAEDIA

Huxley points up a contrast between the real and the actual that highlights the uncanny truthfulness of *Brave New World*. Following 1957, an actual experiment was made in a California penal institution in which an attempt was made to instill good behavior through means of sleep-teaching. In the second chapter of *Brave New World*, the Director of Hatcheries and Conditioning for western Europe explains to some neophytes the working of an identical state-controlled system of ethical education.

The Director goes on to elaborate the philosophy behind this method of moral training. Historically, in the brave new world, the early attempts at hypnopaedia had been ill-founded. Educators had tried unsuccessfully to instill intellectual subject matter, only to find that cerebration tended to interfere with the sleep itself. In order for the sleep teaching to work effectively, the Utopian investigators found that what was taught had to be nonrational. And this proved an unforeseen absolute boon: what could be more antirational than propaganda. No wonder the Director describes true hypnopaedia as "the greatest moralizing and socializing force of all time." Again, one began in childhood, and by the time the child matured he was the embodiment of what he'd been sleep-taught.

Says Huxley, at the present time this kind of experiment is being confined to volunteers in an extraordinarily scrupulous way. But what might happen should some leader of the program decide that volunteers should not remain volunteers?

Well now, just how effective is sleep teaching? Many studies have been conducted, most of them, naturally, concerned with measuring the recollection of the material "taught" during the somnolent state. Business immediately jumped to exploit the "technique," without much basis in fact of the experimental findings. The sale of tape recorders for the purpose skyrocketed. Even the United States Army adopted the method to supplement its diurnal instruction in code and languages. To a lesser extent even the phonograph record was pressed into service, again to play upon the emotional problems and infirmities of the maladjusted or the anxiety ridden. Self-improvement is a big field for hypnopaedia, and its benefactors swear by it.

In order to build some foundation of evidence under this experiential superstructure, one can turn to the encephalograph and watch the actual activity of the brain during sleep teaching. One finds that during light sleep the brain exhibits so-called alpha waves (unlike deep sleep during which it does not), and at such time subjects will accept suggestions as readily as under hypnosis—and we have long known the effectiveness of hypnosis in altering a wide variety of conditions and behavioral patterns.

Children and invalids are particularly suggestible. But just as some people "can't be hypnotized," so there is constitutional variability from individual to individual in reacting to the power of suggestion. Most people are moderately suggestible—in some ways a boon for democracy where for effective self-government, there must be some suggestion and some agreement. But there remains the problem of discriminating the beneficial suggestion from the harmful—the variation in suggestibility and how to account for it.

In a Massachusetts study in the use of placebos, it was found that neither age, gender, nor IQ was a significant factor in degree of suggestibility. The significant factor was found to be a difference in temperament— the feelings of persons toward themselves and toward others. The ones who reacted positively to suggestion were more easygoing and friendly. On the other hand, they also exhibited much anxiety, which was manifested commonly in psychosomatic symptoms. Finally, they tended to be religious.

The incidence of easily suggestible people is far too high for the good of democracy. It puts us *all* at the mercy of subversion from potential mind manipulators. Man's mind is in large part disposed to it; the tools to accomplish it are at hand. We therefore must explore the possibility of educating men into legislating control of this menace to freedom in our time.

CHAPTER XI

EDUCATION FOR FREEDOM

Many of the details of this chapter, as well as of the following, are reiterations. Even Huxley's program of education for freedom has been broached earlier. Nevertheless, together these chapters form a dramatic and impassioned summary followed by a plea for action in the race toward oblivion.

A beginning must be made by stating the facts of man—these must represent the truth about his biology and his environment as accurately as possible; it is from these facts that genuine human values can be made to arise, as will the disclosure of the means for acquiring and safeguarding them. The group espousing the Social Ethic looks upon its members as mirror images of one another: nothing matters but that the same tastes and same pursuits will force the individual into the social mold; hence the group tends to overemphasize the influence of the socio-economic environment. Yet, as Huxley pointed out much earlier, each human being is different by nature—each has his own little idiosyncracies of thinking and acting, and if these are to be given honest expression, we must have freedom, because, as we have seen, nonconformity is seen as a potential danger according to the view of the autocrat.

Once, not too long ago, sociology and psychology were in the throes of behaviorism. The individual's character, as well as his contribution to society, was thought to be part and parcel the product of those forces which that society had imposed upon him. Everyone defended nurture; no one would have dreamed of speaking out in favor of the influence of nature. But today, the pendulum has swung back a good deal, at least in those parts of our world where freedom is valued. Huxley cites William James, "If anything is humanly certain it is that the great man's society, properly so called, does not make him before he can remake it," and Lord Russell to the effect that the causes of historical change are three: economic fluctuation, political science, and outstanding individuals. The individual is the motive force in society; he moves within the larger social organization, but he makes his contributions largely in spite of it. The organization is meant to protect and bring him safely to the point where he can make his individuality felt as a force, and he only needs the social organization thereafter—if it works well—to take care of the myriad mechanical and repetitive functions which would merely sap his personal energies if he had to give thought constantly to every one of them.

This does *not* mean that we have an engraved invitation to sit back and let the organization do everything for us (it will be only too happy to), taking *no* interest in it, and using it as license merely to indulge our whims and fancies and to vegetate in general. That "human infants are born uniform and that individuals are the product of conditioning by and within the collective environment" is still the view of many in our time; in the brave new world, everyone believes it.

Education for freedom will teach infinite biological multiplicity, as well as those ethical precepts which will safeguard that diversity: freedom, tolerance, and cooperation. It will be an education in the proper uses of language, so that good and bad propaganda can be held up against man's true nature as a measuring device. The new student will have to analyze as absurd the myths of demagoguery, while being able to recognize the worth of *some* of the sayings of the "old traditionalists." He will have to be able to recognize value in the new and untried, and much of finding the way to this knowledge he will have to discover within himself. To find the golden mean between utter credulity and a crippling skepticism, he will have to be taught "the old familiar fact, lately rediscovered by modern psychiatry — the fact that, whatever their mental and physical diversity, love is as necessary to human beings as food and shelter; and finally the value of intelligence, without which love is impotent and freedom unattainable."

"Yes," says our imaginary dictator, "you are correct: human beings are not absolutely alike — but they are *enough* alike..."

CHAPTER XII

WHAT CAN BE DONE?

It is a mistake to think that because democracy is mentioned so often it is the hero of this book. The hero is freedom, and democracy is merely its manservant — the best one found yet. The antihero is human ignorance.

But as many of our wisest statesmen have observed we must "work" at freedom just as we must work at thriving at all. The problem of thriving in classical and medieval times was at best to keep the body free from restraint; the problem of our age is to keep the mind unrestrained. The victim of physical captivity is constantly aware of his agony, but the victim of mental captivity may never know discomfort, may — as we have imagined — even welcome and enjoy it. There is time now — but not for long — to educate for collective action by legal means to compel technology and business to work in the interest of freedom, rather than against it. We may in fact uncover a better vehicle for freedom than democracy (but that does not seem very likely).

Behind all this short-term optimism there still lurks the specter of those impersonal forces mentioned at the outset. Men like Huxley have come face to face with their menace and cried out about them. It will take all our wit and all our initiative. Still the impulse must come from within. Will the education for freedom compel us really to want to *act* upon our knowledge? Is it too late for most of us to reacquire an idea of duty? The alternatives are doubtless physical oblivion or spiritual oblivion — perhaps both. Time is working against us and in favor of those impersonal forces; this very moment may be pivotal.

REVIEW QUESTIONS

1. What is Huxley's attitude toward science? How does he contrast it with technology? Do you think such a comparison is common in current literature?

2. Has man *always* written about Utopia? Is there any promise of one being attainable? How is the adjective Utopian used?

3. What is Huxley's attitude toward the flesh? How is this manifested through the actions of the principal characters in *Brave New World?* Do you suppose it relates to his adolescent illness?

4. The civilization Huxley depicts represents the magnification of negative ideals. This kind of society has often been called a Utopia-in-reverse. What does this mean? Is a Utopia-in-reverse more likely to be realized than a Utopia? How many devices might they share in common. Taken on its own terms, is the brave new world without flaws?

5. *Brave New World* has been described by some as a satire of a "hopelessly drifting age." If so, what does the novel satirize? Try to relate the satirized subject or object with its real-world correlative. Do we find irony in the two works under consideration? Paradox?

6. Mystical religion was one of the preoccupations of Huxley's later life. Is there any evidence of its influence in either of the works discussed.

7. In *Point Counter Point,* Huxley discusses two of his literary notions: "the musicalization of fiction" and "the novel of ideas." What do you suppose he means by these? Can you make a case for either or both in the works under consideration?

8. In his earlier novels, Huxley ridiculed the aristocrats and Bohemians of postwar London, who devoted their existences to social

revelry and chit-chat. Show how these same failings in human nature feature in *Brave New World* and *Brave New World Revisited.*

9. In *Brave New World,* what do you think of some of Huxley's devices for mass amusement and control. Describe some. Is there a chance of their invention or discovery?

10. What is prophecy? How good do you think Huxley's prophecies for man's future are? What do we mean when we use the term *visionary?*

11. What are the impersonal forces within man that are pushing him toward the brave new world? What are the symptoms they exhibit? Is there a paradox involved in man's trying to ameliorate his lot?

12. Do you think the brave new world can be prevented? Does Huxley offer a cure for the conditions propelling us toward it?

SELECTED BIBLIOGRAPHY

Bernd, Daniel Walter. *The Search for the Complete Man.* (The development of the hero in the novels of Aldous Huxley.) Lincoln, Neb., 1957.

Brook, Jocelyn. *Aldous Huxley.* New York, London: Longmans Green, 1954.

Joad, Cyril Edwin Mitchinson. *Return to Philosophy.* New York: E. P. Dutton, 1936.

Rolo, Charles J. *The World of Aldous Huxley.* New York: Grosset's Universal Library (paperback), 1947.

Your Guides to Successful Test Preparation.

Cliffs Test Preparation Guides

Efficient preparation means better test scores. Go with the experts and use **Cliffs Test Preparation Guides**. They'll help you reach your goals because they're: • Complete • Concise • Functional • In-depth. They are focused on helping you know what to expect from each test. The test-taking techniques have been proven in classroom programs nationwide.

Recommended for individual use or as a part of formal test preparation programs.